In the closing days of his life, Publius Vergilius Maro (Virgil) wrote these words: *"Fortune favors the bold, but abandons the timid."* Two thousand years later Jeff Sandefer and the Reverend Robert Sirico have written *A Field Guide for the Hero's Journey*. They describe in clear, concise, and cogent stories the way the journey, through **bold choices and actions**, transforms and fulfills life. This life is infused with purpose, freedom, faith, and love. Following the "Guide" on the *Hero's Journey*, you shall transfigure for good, your work, wealth, and wisdom.

—MIKE ANDERSON
Retired CEO of Presbyterian Health Foundation,
former Senior Minister of Westminster
Presbyterian Church, Oklahoma City,
Director of Worldwide Missions
of the United Presbyterian Church

We all need encouragement. *Hero's Journey* is my Book of Encouragement for this year in the same way *Jesus Calling* was for last. Written with brief, powerful stories from the life experiences of two brilliant men at totally opposite ends of the economic spectrum—a multimillionaire entrepreneur and a Catholic Priest, this remarkable work is mostly a mosaic of what the greatest minds of all time had to say about nine themes that lead to a balanced life. The wisdom content is skillfully abridged and excerpted to be all essence. There is not a wasted word. There is profit on every page.

—BOB BUFORD
Founder, Leadership Network,
Author, *Halftime and Finishing Well*

Too many people today believe that a heroic life is only for an elite few. *Hero's Journey* dispels that belief with a realistic and concrete message that a life lived to the highest standards—a hero's life—is for anyone willing to accept the challenge.

—J. C. HUIZENGA
Founder, National Heritage Academies

Many "new ideas" in today's leadership writing are recycled from timeless exemplars in literature, philosophy, and sacred texts. *Hero's Journey* draws upon those texts but wraps them in poignantly personal lessons from a world-class entrepreneur and a worldly statesman priest.

—LOUIS KIM
Vice President, Hewlett-Packard

Jeff Sandefer and Rev. Robert Sirico have national reputations as extraordinary teachers who change the lives of their students forever. Guided by the premise that everyone has the potential to be a hero, this inspirational and practical book will help you focus on the right questions that will enable you to lead a life of purpose, achievement, and, yes, heroism.

—ADAM MEYERSON
President, The Philanthropy Roundtable

A Field Guide for the Hero's Journey is the modern "how-to" for entrepreneurs working on accomplishing big things. Joseph Campbell would be proud. You can't ask for two better guides on this subject.

—ANDREAS WIDMER
author of *The Pope and the CEO*

A FIELD GUIDE FOR THE

HERO'S
JOURNEY

inspirational classics and practical advice from a serial entrepreneur and an entrepreneurial priest

A FIELD GUIDE FOR THE

HERO'S JOURNEY

inspirational classics and practical advice from a serial entrepreneur and an entrepreneurial priest

Jeff Sandefer
Rev. Robert Sirico

Edited and Compiled by Amanda Witt

ACTONINSTITUTE

A Field Guide for the Hero's Journey

© 2012 by Acton Institute

ISBN: 978-1-938948-31-2

British Library Cataloguing in Publication Information Available

Library of Congress Cataloging-in-Publication Data

Jeff Sandefer and Rev. Robert Sirico
   A Field Guide for the Hero's Journey

ACTONINSTITUTE

98 E. Fulton
Grand Rapids, Michigan 49503
Phone: 616.454.3080
Fax: 616.454.9454

Interior composition by Judy Schafer
Cover design by Peter Ho

Printed in the United States of America

CONTENTS

Introduction: Calling All Heroes (Could This Mean You?)   v

1. The First Step   1

    My First Step — Jeff Sandefer   2

    Asking Life's Deep Questions — Rev. Robert Sirico   3

    The Man in the Arena — Theodore Roosevelt   5

    Can't — Edgar A. Guest   6

    Things Not Done Before — Edgar A. Guest   7

    The Lark and Her Young Ones — Aesop   8

    Psalm of Life — Henry Wadsworth Longfellow   9

2. Who Am I, and Who Do I Want to Become?   11

    Misunderstanding Who We Are — Rev. Robert Sirico   12

    Stars and Stepping-Stones — Jeff Sandefer   14

    The Golden Touch — Nathaniel Hawthorne   16

    How Much Land Does a Man Need? — Leo Tolstoy   21

    The Parable of the Talents — Jesus (King James Bible)   25

    Do What You Can — Anonymous   27

    The Lion and the Mouse — Aesop   28

    Apple-Seed John — Jon Chapman and Carolyn S. Bailey   29

    Vocation — Frederick Buechner   31

3. The Importance of Setting Guardrails   35

    A Road Not Taken — Jeff Sandefer   36

    On the Playground — Rev. Robert Sirico   38

    The Fox and the Goat — Aesop   40

Icarus and Daedalus—Josephine Preston Peabody		41
Odysseus and the Sirens—Josephine Preston Peabody		43
Ozymandias—Percy Bysshe Shelley		44
The Emperor of Flower Seeds—Chinese Folktale		45
Sir Thomas More—Rev. Robert Sirico and Amanda Witt		48
When the Nazis Came—Martin Niemöller		50

4. **What Companions Do You Want with You on Your Journey?** 53

The Garden—Rev. Robert Sirico		55
Choose Your Fellow Travelers Well—Jeff Sandefer		56
The Wonderful Wizard of Oz (Excerpt)—L. Frank Baum		57
The Pilgrim's Progress (Excerpted and Abridged)—John Bunyan		59
The Travelers and the Bear—Aesop		61
The Farmer and His Sons—Aesop (retold by James Baldwin)		62
Ecclesiastes 4:9–12—KJV		62
The Lever—Modern Folktale		63

5. **Stones in the Road** 65

Three Kinds of Students—Jeff Sandefer		66
The Persistent Innovator—Rev. Robert Sirico		68
The Farmer's Sons—Aesop		70
The Strenuous Life (Excerpted)—Theodore Roosevelt		71
The Stone in the Road—Sarah Arnold		72
The Crow and the Pitcher—Aesop		73
Excerpts from Three Speeches Given during World War II—Winston Churchill		74

6. **The Giant of Despair** 77

Archbishop Van Thuan—Rev. Robert Sirico		78
Who Would Choose Despair?—Jeff Sandefer		80
The Pilgrim's Progress (Excerpted)—John Bunyan		81
I Have a Dream (Excerpted)—Martin Luther King, Jr.		84
Psalm 23—David		86
Be Like the Bird—Victor Hugo		87
Henry V—William Shakespeare		88

7. Rest   91

    No Rest for the Builders—Jeff Sandefer   93

    Distraction from Distraction—Rev. Robert Sirico   94

    Daffodils—William Wordsworth   96

    Genesis 1:27–2:3 KJV   97

    Psalm 46 KJV   98

    Come, Rest Awhile—Lucy Maud Montgomery   99

    The Pilgrim's Progress—John Bunyan
    (retold by Mary MacGregor)   100

8. Fighting the Dragon   103

    Before the Dragon Arrives—Rev. Robert Sirico   105

    When Will Your Dragon Appear?—Jeff Sandefer   107

    Invictus—William Ernest Henley   109

    Beowulf—Retold by Hamilton Wright Mabie   111

    Give Me Liberty or Give Me Death—Patrick Henry   113

    David and Goliath (Excerpted)—1 Samuel 17 KJV   115

    The American Crisis (Excerpted)—Thomas Paine   118

9. Coming Home   123

    The End Game—Jeff Sandefer   125

    Success—Rev. Robert Sirico   126

    High Flight—John Gillespie Magee, Jr.   128

    And Yet Fools Say—George Sanford Holmes   129

    The Bridge Builder—Will Allen Dromgoole   130

    Crossing the Bar—Alfred, Lord Tennyson   131

    A Farewell—Charles Kingsley   132

Works Cited   135

About the Authors   139

INTRODUCTION

Calling All Heroes
(Could This Mean You?)

D o you feel like something big is missing from your life? Do you feel trapped, bored, stuck in a meaningless routine? It may be you think you're too ordinary to ever do something special. Perhaps you're afraid that if you try, you'll fail.

The startling truth is this: Just about anyone can do great things, can live a life that's remarkable, purposeful, excellent, and yes, even heroic. If you want to be a hero, you can be.

How?

That's what this book is all about.

We—Father Robert Sirico (a priest) and Jeff Sandefer (an entrepreneur)—have been in your shoes. We have heard the whisper of a calling, yet turned away. We've struck out on epic challenges only to fail, sometimes miserably. But we've also picked ourselves up and tried again and have succeeded, sometimes spectacularly.

We've watched others make the journey as well. We've walked alongside saints and demons. We've seen what unchecked success can do to a soul.

We have since taught, led, and counseled hundreds of people who want meaningful lives, people who want to leave a mark on the world. And we've done so because we believe that heroes are not born, but made. The journey is never easy. If it were, it wouldn't be heroic—but it can be done.

Will you choose to do it? Will you decide to journey heroically, instead of spending your life merely marking time?

We hope so. Our world desperately needs heroic people—people who shape events, who act rather than watch, who are creative and brave. Such people are needed in every field, in every realm of life—not only in law enforcement and disaster response but also in science, education, business and finance, health care, the arts, journalism, agriculture, and—not least—in the home.

Wherever you are, whatever you do, you can learn to live heroically. You might not ever be called to save a child from a burning building, but you can become the sort of person who is willing to do that or other heroic deeds, and with the willingness will come the opportunities. You can choose a life that's meaningful. You can make a difference and succeed, and do so heroically.

How?

First, by contemplating the heroic journey. Read our own stories. Read the classic tales and poems we have chosen to illustrate the promises and perils of each step. Then, think about your own heroic journey by working through the "ask this" questions we provide at the end of each chapter. These questions are designed to help you apply each lesson to your own life.

Finally, move from thinking to acting by implementing the practical "try this" suggestions we make—suggestions we have followed ourselves in our quest to live heroically.

Will these simple steps work? Yes, if you're committed to becoming heroic. They will set your feet firmly on the path. They will open your eyes to the right direction. They will warn you of pitfalls, and teach you how to avoid them.

Simple steps like these work because the heroic path is, essentially, about making small choices that add up to a big life.

A life in which you make a difference—in yourself, in others, in the world.

A life in which you forgive yourself for your trespasses, knowing that you've learned from them, and in which you forgive the trespasses of others.

A life in which you close your eyes for the last time without regret, confident that you took the hours and days and years you were given and made something spectacular out of them.

Does that sound like something you want?

If so, this is the book for you. Welcome to your heroic journey.

1

THE FIRST STEP

Nike's ad campaign "Just Do It!" has been so effective because it recognizes a natural human tension. We all feel an urge to excel, to reach beyond our confinements and transcend ourselves. But we're also plagued by inertia. This inertia is the first and biggest obstacle to success.

If we're having trouble getting up the gumption to *do something*, we need to consider and control the way we think—the way we think in general about our world, but more specifically and more intimately, the way we think about ourselves. Do we see ourselves as merely passive biological entities that are essentially acted upon from without? Or do we understand that we are beings of august dignity who possess meaning and purpose in this world and within our nature—a sense of calling and vocation?

If you want to be a hero, you must decide to be a person who acts, rather than a person who says "I can't." You *can*. You can make deliberate choices that will change your life. You can take steps—many small ones, occasionally a big one—toward your chosen goal, your star, your grail.

Do you want to move in a meaningful direction? Do you want to do remarkable things and become a remarkable person? Are you ready, as the old U.S. Army commercials put it, to "be all that you can be"?

Then do more than wish. Commit yourself, body and soul, to finding and following your heroic path.

MY FIRST STEP

Jeff Sandefer

My first step toward an entrepreneurial calling began with my burning desire for air conditioning.

As a teenager, my father wisely insisted that I work summers as a laborer in the oil fields, under an unrelenting West Texas sun. I hated what seemed like meaningless manual labor, the bullying and the boasting conversations about sex, drugs, and alcohol. But most of all I hated the relentless heat, which started at dawn and made even the wind feel like a blast furnace.

To me, heaven was the inside of an air-conditioned pickup truck, the spot reserved for a foreman, a spot no one was going to give to a teenage boy.

But as I went on with my sweaty work, longing to sit in that position of air-conditioned power, I began to notice things. First, I noticed that all the heavy equipment lying around wasn't needed for the light painting and clean-up work that occupied most of our time, but was nonetheless charged to customers. Then I noticed that my fellow laborers, paid by the hour, had little incentive do anything other than shirk work and wait for quitting time to come.

So I formed a plan to get into air conditioning. I partnered with my best friend and we convinced our high school football coaches to go to work for us. They contributed the use of their pickup trucks to haul painting equipment, and we agreed to pay them by the job, not the hour. They, in turn, hired their football players to work for them, and paid them the same way. My job became finding customers and overseeing the work. My partner handled the operations.

The hourly workers painted a large metal storage tank in three days. Our crews arrived at dawn, painted until dark, and could finish three tanks a day—a ninefold-productivity gain.

I was seventeen that summer, and my best friend and I made $100,000. More importantly, I got to spend most of my time in air conditioning.

Yes, it's more dramatic to see a blinding flash like Saul did on the road to Damascus. But whether you start your journey with a flash of light or by finally listening to that still small voice or by running away from a job you hate, what is important is to take that first step so that you'll never be counted among those whom Teddy Roosevelt called the "cold and timid souls who know neither victory nor defeat."

ASKING LIFE'S DEEP QUESTIONS

Rev. Robert Sirico

People who do not know me or the personal odyssey I went through to come the point in my life where I responded to a call to the priesthood naturally tend to think that I was raised in a pious home of regular churchgoers.

I admire brother-priests who fit this profile and the stability of clear purpose many of them have felt all their lives. But that was not me. I had an interest in religion as a child, but in the midst of this interest—indeed this intense quest—I still felt personally unsatisfied. Some piece was missing. I always had a proclivity to ask the "hard questions," which were often uncomfortable questions. I went looking for answers, and that search brought me in contact with ideas, places, people, and movements I otherwise never would have entertained.

One particular memory at the beginning of that search sticks in my mind. Imagine a teenage Catholic boy going up to a rectory door in the early 1960s and asking the Irish housekeeper to speak with a priest.

"Father," I said to the priest when he came. "How can we as Catholics believe...." And I began to pelt the young priest with what I thought to be profound theological insights. I cannot recall the details of those inquiries now, almost a half century later, but I do recall the answer the priest gave.

"Look, I am a busy man and your questions tell me that you are much too religious. You don't want to become a fanatic, now do you? I suggest that rather than getting into these kinds of matters, you go home and read *Huckleberry Finn*, or something like that."

For the life of me I could not understand what *Huckleberry Finn* had to do with anything, but I knew when my concerns were being dismissed.

I did read *Huckleberry Finn* and, of late, have come to a deeper understanding of what that encounter with the priest meant in my life. Here are some of the conclusions that I have drawn from it:

The first is that some advisers and mentors do not understand that other people's burning desire to have great dreams of meaning and significance in their lives may not match up with their ability to formulate their questions. Very often people ask profound questions under the guise of confusion, imprecision, and (in my case) precociousness.

3

A second thing I have come to understand is that it is very rare that one single answer provides the whole key to the puzzle we are looking to solve.

And finally, it may very well be the case that advice we are given that is intended to dismiss us, or that fails to appreciate a striving for a heroic ideal, may yet contain some valuable gem. After all, didn't Huck's untutored brain formulate some tough questions about his racist society and lead to a radical answer?

To a very great extent we have lost the sense of the heroic quest in our culture. It is the "anti-hero" who is so often celebrated in contemporary novels or films and the "bad boy" non-achiever who gets the girl in the end. It was not always so, and need not be today.

THE MAN IN THE ARENA *(Abridged)*

Theodore Roosevelt (1858-1919)

It is not the critic who counts; not the man who points out how the strong man stumbles, or where the doer of deeds could have done them better. The credit belongs to the man who is actually in the arena, whose face is marred by dust and sweat and blood; who strives valiantly; who errs, who comes short again and again, because there is no effort without error and shortcoming; but who does actually strive to do the deeds; who knows great enthusiasms, the great devotions; who spends himself in a worthy cause; who at the best knows in the end the triumph of high achievement, and who at the worst, if he fails, at least fails while daring greatly, so that his place shall never be with those cold and timid souls who neither know victory nor defeat.

Some of us are natural optimists, and some natural pessimists. We can, however, work to mitigate our tendencies. Optimists can learn a little caution, and pessimists can school themselves to hope.

CAN'T

Edgar A. Guest (1881-1959)

Can't is the worst word that's written or spoken;
Doing more harm here than slander and lies;
On it is many a strong spirit broken,
And with it many a good purpose dies.
It springs from the lips of the thoughtless each morning
And robs us of courage we need through the day:
It rings in our ears like a timely-sent warning
And laughs when we falter and fall by the way.

Can't is the father of feeble endeavor,
The parent of terror and half-hearted work;
It weakens the efforts of artisans clever,
And makes of the toiler an indolent shirk.
It poisons the soul of the man with a vision,
It stifles in infancy many a plan;
It greets honest toiling with open derision
And mocks at the hopes and the dreams of a man.

Can't is a word none should speak without blushing;
To utter it should be a symbol of shame;
Ambition and courage it daily is crushing;
It blights a man's purpose and shortens his aim.
Despise it with all of your hatred of error;
Refuse it the lodgment it seeks in your brain;
Arm against it as a creature of terror,
And all that you dream of you some day shall gain.

Can't is the word that is foe to ambition,
An enemy ambushed to shatter your will;
Its prey is forever the man with a mission
And bows but to courage and patience and skill.
Hate it, with hatred that's deep and undying,
For once it is welcomed 'twill break any man;
Whatever the goal you are seeking, keep trying
And answer this demon by saying: "I can."

Dare to dream.

THINGS NOT DONE BEFORE

Edgar A. Guest (1881-1959)

The things that haven't been done before,
Those are the things to try;
Columbus dreamed of an unknown shore
At the rim of the far-flung sky,
And his heart was bold and his faith was strong
As he ventured in dangers new,
And he paid no heed to the jeering throng
Or the fears of the doubting crew.

The many will follow the beaten track
With guideposts on the way,
They live and have lived for ages back
With a chart for every day.
Someone has told them it's safe to go
On the road he has traveled o'er,
And all that they ever strive to know
Are the things that were known before.

A few strike out, without map or chart,
Where never a man has been,
From the beaten paths they draw apart
To see what no man has seen.
There are deeds they hunger alone to do;
Though battered and bruised and sore,
They blaze the path for the many,
Who do nothing not done before.

The things that haven't been done before
Are the tasks worth while to-day;
Are you one of the flock that follows,
Or are you one that shall lead the way?
Are you one of the timid souls that quail
At the jeers of a doubting crew,
Or dare you, whether you win or fail,
Strike out for a goal that's new.

Are you willing to be the one who sets to work in order to make good things happen, instead of always waiting for someone else to be the instigator?

THE LARK AND HER YOUNG ONES

Aesop (circa 620-560 BC)

A Lark made her nest in a field of young wheat. As the days passed, the wheat stalks grew tall and the young birds, too, grew in strength. Then one day, when the ripe golden grain waved in the breeze, the Farmer and his son came into the field.

"This wheat is now ready for reaping," said the Farmer. "We must call in our neighbors and friends to help us harvest it."

The young Larks in their nest close by were much frightened, for they knew they would be in great danger if they did not leave the nest before the reapers came. When the Mother Lark returned with food for them, they told her what they had heard.

"Do not be frightened, children," said the Mother Lark. "If the Farmer said he would call in his neighbors and friends to help him do his work, this wheat will not be reaped for a while yet."

A few days later, the wheat was so ripe, that when the wind shook the stalks, a hail of wheat grains came rustling down on the young Larks' heads.

"If this wheat is not harvested at once," said the Farmer, "we shall lose half the crop. We cannot wait any longer for help from our friends. Tomorrow we must set to work, ourselves."

When the young Larks told their mother what they had heard that day, she said:

"Then we must be off at once. When a man decides to do his own work and not depend on anyone else, then you may be sure there will be no more delay."

There was much fluttering and trying out of wings that afternoon, and at sunrise next day, when the Farmer and his son cut down the grain, they found an empty nest.

PSALM OF LIFE

Henry Wadsworth Longfellow (1807-1882)

What the heart of the young man said to the psalmist—

Tell me not, in mournful numbers,
Life is but an empty dream!—
For the soul is dead that slumbers,
And things are not what they seem.

Life is real! Life is earnest!
And the grave is not its goal;
Dust thou art, to dust returnest,
Was not spoken of the soul.

Not enjoyment, and not sorrow,
Is our destined end or way;
But to act, that each to-morrow
Find us farther than to-day.

Art is long, and Time is fleeting,
And our hearts, though stout and brave,
Still, like muffled drums, are beating
Funeral marches to the grave.

In the world's broad field of battle,
In the bivouac of Life,
Be not like dumb, driven cattle!
Be a hero in the strife!

Trust no Future, howe'er pleasant!
Let the dead Past bury its dead!
Act,—act in the living Present!
Heart within, and God o'erhead!

Lives of great men all remind us
We can make our lives sublime,
And, departing, leave behind us
Footprints on the sands of time;

Footprints, that perhaps another,
Sailing o'er life's solemn main,
A forlorn and shipwrecked brother,
Seeing, shall take heart again.

Let us, then, be up and doing,
With a heart for any fate;
Still achieving, still pursuing,
Learn to labor and to wait.

Ask This

Do you need a grand, detailed, complete plan before you can begin your hero's journey? Has this become an excuse for never taking the first step?

What is the first step in starting your hero's journey?

How can looking outside of yourself, beyond yourself, help you begin a quest?

How could feeling sorry for yourself prevent you from setting out on a quest?

How can cultivating an attitude of gratitude or of "counting your blessings" help on a long journey?

Are you ready to stop any negative chatter in your thoughts, and replace it with a vision of possibility and achievement?

Are you ready to commit to living heroically?

Try This

As you begin your hero's journey, you might want to keep a journal of your progress. This allows you time to reflect on where you have come from and where you are going. Keeping a journal has been shown to have a long-term positive effect on happiness, satisfaction, and fulfillment. So does meditation and prayer.

2

WHO AM I, AND WHO DO I WANT TO BECOME?

We frequently ask children, "What do you want to be when you grow up?" Many adults have a similar question lurking in the backs of their minds. But that is really beginning at the wrong end. First we should ask, "Who am I?"

Our personalities and desires shape our callings. There is something embedded in each of us that, without robbing us of our freedom, nonetheless prods or tugs us in the optimal direction.

So, when you embark upon a heroic journey—a life filled with meaning and purpose—the first step is to heed the admonition inscribed over the entrance to the Oracle of Delphi in ancient Greece: "Know Thyself." Search out who you are, and then you will be equipped to discover your heroic calling.

Assess your personality, your natural talents and earned skills, your interests and beliefs, your strengths and weaknesses. Be open to the observations and reflections of others in a nondefensive way.

Once you have a good read on who you are right now, you can begin to consider who you want to become.

MISUNDERSTANDING WHO WE ARE

Rev. Robert Sirico

In the early 1970s the world was awash in movements of all sorts: spiritual, musical, political, and cultural. It seemed the whole world was being turned upside down and a new, hopeful, and utopian horizon was in the offing. In my own personal journey I found myself in the middle of much of this ambience.

One day, coming in from a round of picketing and sit-ins, a group of friends gathered in the living room of my small apartment just off Hollywood Boulevard. As we sat there recounting the day, we spoke of our hopes—even if to my mind now, too simplistically and idealistically—of what the world would be like "when the revolution comes."

One after another we spoke of our dreams passionately, laughingly. When my turn came I said, "When the revolution comes, we'll all shop at Gucci's."

I was greeted with bewilderment by my jean-clad, Birkenstocked, and patchouli-oil scented comrades. My friend Ann, a radical feminist Trotskyite sitting (appropriately) to my left looked over and said,

"Gucci's, Robert?"

"What? We are working for the redistribution of the wealth, aren't we? Gucci's is a metaphor for a time when everyone will be able to buy quality goods and services at accessible prices." That was my argument.

Silence.

Then Ann again, "But Gucci's? I don't think you are a real socialist."

How often do we, by an unplanned word or action or choice, reveal our true selves—if not to ourselves immediately, then to those keen observers who know us best?

That perceptive one-word question Ann asked of me that summer day cut to the heart of my identity, of who I thought I was. And it stuck with me over the coming years, even as a transformation of self-awareness began to take shape. Initially this began with reading some books on economics that helped me discover that the fundamental error of my socialism was anthropological in nature: It misunderstood human beings in their need to be creative and free.

The trajectory of ideas that this would lead me on would return me to some of the earliest assumptions I'd learned at home and in the faith I learned as a child from the sisters in those catechism classes about human dignity and transcendence.

STARS AND STEPPING-STONES

Jeff Sandefer

Entrepreneurs are driven by action. Introspection, if it comes, comes later. That's why we are so easily captured by the shiny trinkets of the Rat Race and the never-ending climb toward unlimited power and meaningless success. In focusing on these outward trappings of success we often forget who we are and where we came from.

Yes, being rich has it rewards. But I regularly move in the circles of the super rich, and trust me, in many cases you wouldn't want to change places with them, not for all the money in the world. Edwin Arlington Robinson got it right in his poem "Richard Cory":

> Whenever Richard Cory went to town,
> We people on the pavement looked at him:
> He was a gentleman from sole to crown,
> Clean favored, and imperially slim.
>
> And he was always quietly arrayed,
> And he was always human when he talked;
> But still he fluttered pulses when he said,
> "Good morning," and he glittered when he walked.
>
> And he was rich—yes, richer than a king,
> And admirably schooled in every grace:
> In fine, we thought that he was everything
> To make us wish that we were in his place.
>
> So on we worked, and waited for the light,
> And went without the meat, and cursed the bread;
> And Richard Cory, one calm summer night,
> Went home and put a bullet in his head.

It's not wealth *per se* that destroys people; but wealth without understanding does. Money—or any kind of success—brings its own set of temptations and pitfalls.

So how can you be prepared? How can you gain some perspective?

I challenge my students to seek "Stars and Stepping-Stones" conversations with potential role models who are further ahead on the journey.

Here's what I tell them: Choose ten people, three under forty but older than you; three between forty and sixty; and at least three over the age of sixty. (You would adjust these numbers, of course, depending on your own age.) Then for at least two hours, interview them about their lives, asking about victories and defeats, triumphs and regrets, and most importantly, the questions they wish they'd asked at your age.

Be willing to learn from their mistakes; be willing to listen to their wisdom. Soak up some much-needed perspective for your journey—seek "stars" that will keep you oriented and heading in the right direction. Seek practical, realistic "stepping-stones" that might lead to your next adventure.

Most of all, remember that these people can help you consider who you are, and who you want to become—something beyond money, power and fame.

Because no matter how big the house or jet plane or yacht, the winner of the Rat Race is still a rat.

What does this saying mean: "The love of money is the root of all evil." Or this: "Money makes a good slave but a poor master."

THE GOLDEN TOUCH *(Abridged)*

Nathaniel Hawthorne (1804–1861)

Once upon a time, there lived a very rich man, and a king besides, whose name was Midas; and he had a little daughter named Marygold.

This King Midas was fonder of gold than of anything else in the world. If he loved anything better, or half so well, it was the one little maiden who played so merrily around her father's footstool. But the more Midas loved his daughter, the more did he desire and seek for wealth. He thought, foolish man, that the best thing he could possibly do for this dear child would be to bequeath her the immensest pile of yellow, glistening coin that had ever been heaped together since the world was made. Thus, he gave all his thoughts and all his time to this one purpose.

Midas was enjoying himself in his treasure-room, one day, as usual, when he perceived a shadow fall over the heaps of gold; and, looking suddenly up, what should he behold but the figure of a stranger.

"You are a wealthy man, friend Midas!" the stranger observed.

"I have done pretty well,—pretty well," answered Midas, in a discontented tone.

"What!" exclaimed the stranger. "Then you are not satisfied? Then what would satisfy you?"

Midas thought a moment. "I wish everything that I touch to be changed to gold!"

The stranger's smile grew very broad. "Be it as you wish, then," he replied. "To-morrow, at sunrise, you will find yourself gifted with the Golden Touch."

In the morning Midas started up, in a kind of joyful frenzy, and ran about the room, grasping at everything that happened to be in his way. He seized one of the bed-posts, and it became immediately a fluted golden pillar. He pulled aside a window-curtain, in order to admit a clear spectacle of the wonders which he was performing; and the tassel grew heavy in his hand,—a mass of gold. He took up a book from the table. At his first touch, it assumed the appearance of such a splendidly bound and gilt-edged volume as one often meets with, nowadays; but, on running his fingers through the leaves, behold! it was a bundle of thin golden plates, in which all the wisdom of the book had grown illegible.

He hurriedly put on his clothes, and was enraptured to see himself in a magnificent suit of gold cloth, which retained its flexibility and softness, although it burdened him a little with its weight. He drew out his handkerchief, which little Marygold had hemmed for him. That was likewise gold, with the dear child's neat and pretty stitches running all along the border, in gold thread!

Somehow or other, this last transformation did not quite please King Midas. He would rather that his little daughter's handiwork should have remained just the same as when she climbed his knee and put it into his hand. But it was not worthwhile to vex himself about a trifle.

Wise King Midas went down stairs, and smiled, on observing that the balustrade of the staircase became a bar of burnished gold. He lifted the doorlatch (it was brass only a moment ago, but golden when his fingers quitted it), and emerged into the garden. Here, as it happened, he found a great number of beautiful roses in full bloom, and others in all the stages of lovely bud and blossom. Their delicate blush was one of the fairest sights in the world; so gentle, so modest, and so full of sweet tranquility, did these roses seem to be.

But Midas knew a way to make them far more precious, according to his way of thinking, so he took great pains in going from bush to bush. By the time this good work was completed, King Midas was summoned to breakfast.

There he heard little Marygold coming along the passageway crying bitterly. This circumstance surprised him, because Marygold was one of the cheerfullest little people whom you would see in a summer's day.

"Pray what is the matter with you, this bright morning?" cried Midas.

Marygold, without taking the apron from her eyes, held out her hand, in which was one of the roses which Midas had so recently transmuted.

"Beautiful!" exclaimed her father. "And what is there in this magnificent golden rose to make you cry?"

"Ah, dear father!" answered the child, as well as her sobs would let her; "All the beautiful roses, that smelled so sweetly and had so many lovely blushes, are blighted and spoilt! They are grown quite yellow, as you see this one, and have no longer any fragrance! What can have been the matter with them?"

"Poh, my dear little girl,—pray don't cry about it!" said Midas, who was ashamed to confess that he himself had wrought the change which so greatly afflicted her. "Sit down and eat your bread and milk."

Midas poured out a cup of coffee, and, as a matter of course, the coffee-pot, whatever metal it may have been when he took it up, was gold when he set it down. He lifted a spoonful of coffee to his lips, and, sipping it, was astonished to perceive that, the instant his lips touched the liquid, it became molten gold, and, the next moment, hardened into a lump!

"Ha!" exclaimed Midas, rather aghast.

"What is the matter, father?" asked little Marygold, gazing at him, with the tears still standing in her eyes.

"What is the matter, father?"

"Nothing, child, nothing!" said Midas. "I don't quite see," thought he to himself, "how I am to get any breakfast!" Hoping that, by dint of great dispatch, he might avoid what he now felt to be a considerable inconvenience, King Midas next snatched a hot potato, and attempted to cram it into his mouth, and swallow it in a hurry. But he found his mouth full of solid metal, which so burnt his tongue that he roared aloud.

"Father, dear father!" cried little Marygold, "Have you burnt your mouth?"

"Ah, dear child," groaned Midas, dolefully, "I don't know what is to become of your poor father!"

With a sweet and sorrowful impulse to comfort him, our little Marygold started from her chair, and, running to Midas, threw her arms affectionately about his knees.

"My precious, precious Marygold!" cried he.

But Marygold made no answer.

Oh, terrible misfortune! The victim of his insatiable desire for wealth, little Marygold was a human child no longer, but a golden statue!

It would be too sad a story, if I were to tell you how Midas, in the fullness of all his gratified desires, began to wring his hands and bemoan himself; and how he could neither bear to look at Marygold, nor yet to look away from her. While he was in this tumult of despair, he suddenly beheld a stranger standing near the door.

"Well, friend Midas," said the stranger, "pray how do you succeed with the Golden Touch?"

Midas shook his head. "I am very miserable," said he.

"Very miserable, indeed!" exclaimed the stranger. "Have you not every-thing that your heart desired?"

"Gold is not everything," answered Midas. "And I have lost all that my heart really cared for."

"Ah! So you have made a discovery, since yesterday?" observed the stranger. "Let us see, then. Which of these two things do you think is really worth the most—the gift of the Golden Touch, or one cup of clear cold water?"

"O blessed water!" exclaimed Midas. "It will never moisten my parched throat again!"

"The Golden Touch," continued the stranger, "or a crust of bread?"

"A piece of bread," answered Midas, "is worth all the gold on earth!"

"The Golden Touch," asked the stranger, "or your own little Marygold, warm, soft, and loving as she was an hour ago?"

"Oh my child, my dear child!" cried poor Midas wringing his hands. "I would not have given that one small dimple in her chin for the power of changing this whole big earth into a solid lump of gold!"

"You are wiser than you were, King Midas!" said the stranger, look-ing seriously at him. "Your own heart, I perceive, has not been entirely changed from flesh to gold. Tell me, now, do you sincerely desire to rid yourself of this Golden Touch?"

"It is hateful to me!" replied Midas.

"Go, then," said the stranger, "and plunge into the river that glides past the bottom of your garden. Take likewise a vase of the same water, and sprinkle it over any object that you may desire to change back again from gold into its former substance. If you do this in earnestness and sincerity, it may possibly repair the mischief which your avarice has occasioned."

You will easily believe that Midas lost no time in snatching up a great earthen pitcher (but, alas me! it was no longer earthen after he touched it), and hastening to the river-side. On reaching the river's brink, he plunged headlong in, without waiting so much as to pull off his shoes. As he dipped the pitcher into the water, it gladdened his very heart to see it change from gold into the same good, honest earthen vessel which it had been before he touched it. He was conscious, also, of a change within himself. A cold, hard, and heavy weight seemed to have gone out of his bosom.

King Midas hastened back to the palace. The first thing he did, as you need hardly be told, was to sprinkle it by handfuls over the golden figure of little Marygold.

"Pray do not, dear father!" cried she. "See how you have wet my nice frock!" For Marygold did not know that she had been a little golden statue; nor could she remember anything that had happened since the moment when she ran with outstretched arms to comfort poor King Midas.

Her father did not think it necessary to tell his beloved child how very foolish he had been, but contented himself with showing how much wiser he had now grown. For this purpose, he led little Marygold into the garden, where he sprinkled all the remainder of the water over the rose-bushes, and with such good effect that above five thousand roses recovered their beautiful bloom.

When does the desire to expand and flourish become a destructive obsession?

HOW MUCH LAND DOES A MAN NEED? *(Abridged)*

Leo Tolstoy (1828-1910)

[*Pahom, a peasant, begins buying land as he is able. He wants to accumulate as much land as he possibly can. He learns that in a remote part of Russia, the Chief of the Bashkirs is selling off parcels of land "by the day. As much as you can go round on your feet in a day is yours, and the price is one thousand roubles a day." Pahom agrees to these wonderfully generous terms, and the Chief tells Pahom to dig holes to mark his boundaries as he goes.*]

The Chief took off his fox-fur cap, placed it on the ground and said: "This will be the mark. Start from here, and return here again. All the land you go round shall be yours."

Pahom started walking neither slowly nor quickly. After having gone a thousand yards he stopped, dug a hole and placed pieces of turf one on another to make it more visible. Then he went on; and now that he had walked off his stiffness he quickened his pace. After a while he dug another hole.

Pahom looked back. The hillock could be distinctly seen in the sunlight, with the people on it, and the glittering tires of the cartwheels. At a rough guess Pahom concluded that he had walked three miles. It was growing warmer; he took off his under-coat, flung it across his shoulder, and went on again. It had grown quite warm now; he looked at the sun, it was time to think of breakfast.

"The first shift is done, but there are four in a day, and it is too soon yet to turn. But I will just take off my boots," said he to himself.

He sat down, took off his boots, stuck them into his girdle, and went on. It was easy walking now.

"I will go on for another three miles," thought he, "and then turn to the left. The spot is so fine, that it would be a pity to lose it. The further one goes, the better the land seems."

He went straight on for a while, and when he looked round, the hillock was scarcely visible and the people on it looked like black ants, and he could just see something glistening there in the sun.

"Ah," thought Pahom, "I have gone far enough in this direction, it is time to turn. Besides I am in a regular sweat, and very thirsty."

He stopped, dug a large hole, and heaped up pieces of turf. Next he untied his flask, had a drink, and then turned sharply to the left. He went on and on; the grass was high, and it was very hot.

Pahom began to grow tired: he looked at the sun and saw that it was noon.

"Well," he thought, "I must have a rest."

He sat down, and ate some bread and drank some water; but he did not lie down, thinking that if he did he might fall asleep. After sitting a little while, he went on again. At first he walked easily: the food had strengthened him; but it had become terribly hot, and he felt sleepy; still he went on, thinking: "An hour to suffer, a life-time to live."

He went a long way in this direction also, and was about to turn to the left again, when he perceived a damp hollow: "It would be a pity to leave that out," he thought. "Flax would do well there." So he went on past the hollow, and dug a hole on the other side of it before he turned the corner. Pahom looked towards the hillock. The heat made the air hazy: it seemed to be quivering, and through the haze the people on the hillock could scarcely be seen.

"Ah!" thought Pahom, "I have made the sides too long; I must make this one shorter." And he went along the third side, stepping faster. He looked at the sun: it was nearly half way to the horizon, and he had not yet done two miles of the third side of the square. He was still ten miles from the goal.

"No," he thought, "though it will make my land lopsided, I must hurry back in a straight line now. I might go too far, and as it is I have a great deal of land."

So Pahom hurriedly dug a hole and went straight towards the hillock, but he now walked with difficulty. He was done up with the heat, his bare feet were cut and bruised, and his legs began to fail. He longed to rest, but it was impossible if he meant to get back before sunset. The sun waits for no man, and it was sinking lower and lower.

"Oh dear," he thought, "if only I have not blundered trying for too much! What if I am too late?"

He looked towards the hillock and at the sun. He was still far from his goal, and the sun was already near the rim. Pahom walked on and on; it was very hard walking, but he went quicker and quicker. He pressed on, but was still far from the place. He began running, threw away his coat, his boots, his flask, and his cap, and kept only the spade that he used as a support.

"What shall I do," he thought again, "I have grasped too much, and ruined the whole affair. I can't get there before the sun sets."

And this fear made him still more breathless. Pahom went on running, his soaking shirt and trousers stuck to him, and his mouth was parched. His breast was working like a blacksmith's bellows, his heart was beating like a hammer, and his legs were giving way as if they did not belong to him. Pahom was seized with terror lest he should die of the strain.

Though afraid of death, he could not stop. "After having run all that way they will call me a fool if I stop now," thought he. And he ran on and on, and drew near and heard the Bashkirs yelling and shouting to him, and their cries inflamed his heart still more. He gathered his last strength and ran on.

The sun was close to the rim, and cloaked in mist looked large, and red as blood. Now, yes now, it was about to set! The sun was quite low, but he was also quite near his aim. Pahom could already see the people on the hillock waving their arms to hurry him up. He could see the fox-fur cap on the ground, and the money on it, and the Chief sitting on the ground holding his sides. And Pahom remembered his dream.

"There is plenty of land," thought he, "but will God let me live on it? I have lost my life, I have lost my life! I shall never reach that spot!"

Pahom looked at the sun, which had reached the earth: one side of it had already disappeared. With all his remaining strength he rushed on, bending his body forward so that his legs could hardly follow fast enough to keep him from falling. Just as he reached the hillock it suddenly grew dark. He looked up—the sun had already set. He gave a cry: "All my labor has been in vain," thought he, and was about to stop, but he heard the Bashkirs still shouting, and remembered that though to him, from below, the sun seemed to have set, they on the hillock could still see it. He took a long breath and ran up the hillock. It was still light there. He reached the top and saw the cap. Before it sat the Chief laughing and holding his sides. Again Pahom remembered his dream, and he uttered a cry: his legs gave way beneath him, he fell forward and reached the cap with his hands.

"Ah, what a fine fellow!" exclaimed the Chief. "He has gained much land!"

Pahom's servant came running up and tried to raise him, but he saw that blood was flowing from his mouth. Pahom was dead!

The Bashkirs clicked their tongues to show their pity.

His servant picked up the spade and dug a grave long enough for Pahom to lie in, and buried him in it. Six feet from his head to his heels was all he needed.

This classic parable is, at first blush, about using money well. Yet can it not also be read as a story about using whatever resources one has—money, skills, talents, connections—rather than being too timid to ever venture out and use them?

THE PARABLE OF THE TALENTS

Jesus

Matthew 25:14–30

King James Version

Note: A talent was a weight of precious metal worth enough to pay a day laborer for twenty years.

For the kingdom of heaven is as a man travelling into a far country, who called his own servants, and delivered unto them his goods. And unto one he gave five talents, to another two, and to another one; to every man according to his several ability; and straightway took his journey.

Then he that had received the five talents went and traded with the same, and made them other five talents. And likewise he that had received two, he also gained other two. But he that had received one went and digged in the earth, and hid his lord's money.

After a long time the lord of those servants cometh, and reckoneth with them. And so he that had received five talents came and brought other five talents, saying, Lord, thou deliveredst unto me five talents: behold, I have gained beside them five talents more.

His lord said unto him, Well done, thou good and faithful servant: thou hast been faithful over a few things, I will make thee ruler over many things: enter thou into the joy of thy lord.

He also that had received two talents came and said, Lord, thou deliveredst unto me two talents: behold, I have gained two other talents beside them.

His lord said unto him, Well done, good and faithful servant; thou hast been faithful over a few things, I will make thee ruler over many things: enter thou into the joy of thy lord.

Then he which had received the one talent came and said, Lord, I knew thee that thou art an hard man, reaping where thou hast not sown, and gathering where thou hast not strawed: And I was afraid, and went and hid thy talent in the earth: lo, there thou hast that is thine.

His lord answered and said unto him, Thou wicked and slothful servant, thou knewest that I reap where I sowed not, and gather where I have not strawed: Thou oughtest therefore to have put my money to the exchangers, and then at my coming I should have received mine own with usury.

Take therefore the talent from him, and give it unto him which hath ten talents. For unto every one that hath shall be given, and he shall have abundance: but from him that hath not shall be taken away even that which he hath.

And cast ye the unprofitable servant into outer darkness: there shall be weeping and gnashing of teeth.

And what if you feel that you have very few resources?

DO WHAT YOU CAN

Anonymous

There was once a farmer who had a large field of corn. He harrowed it and weeded it with the greatest care, for he wanted to sell the corn and buy good things for his family with the money. But after he had worked hard, he saw the corn wither and droop, for no rain fell, and he began to fear that he was to have no crop. He felt very sad, and every morning he went out to the field and looked at the thirsty stalks and wished for the rain to fall.

One day, as he stood looking up at the sky, two little raindrops saw him, and one said to the other: "Look at that farmer. I feel very sorry for him. He took such pains with his field of corn, and now it is drying up. I wish I might help him."

"Yes," said the other, "but you are only a little raindrop. What can you do? You can't wet even one hill."

"Well," said the first, "I know, to be sure, I cannot do much; but perhaps I can cheer the farmer a little, and I am going to do my best. I'll go to the field to show my good will, if I can't do anything more. Here I go!"

The first raindrop had no sooner started for the field than the second one said:

"Well, if you really insist upon going, I think I will go, too. Here I come!" And down went the raindrops. One came—pat—on the farmer's nose, and one fell on a thirsty stalk of corn.

"Dear me," said the farmer, "what's that? A raindrop! Where did it come from? I do believe we shall have a shower."

By this time a great many raindrops had come together to see what all the commotion was about.

When they saw the two kind little drops going down to cheer the farmer, and water his corn, one said: "If you two are going on such a good errand, I'll go, too!" And down he came. "And I!" said another. "And I!" And so said they all, until a whole shower came and the corn was watered. Then the corn grew and ripened—all because one little raindrop tried to do what it could.

If you are convinced you are a mouse surrounded by stronger and more impressive people, ask yourself, "What can I do that these mighty lions can't do?"

THE LION AND THE MOUSE

Aesop (circa 620–560 BC)

Once when a lion was asleep a little mouse began running up and down upon him; this soon wakened the lion, who placed his huge paw upon him, and opened his big jaws to swallow him.

"Pardon, O King," cried the little mouse: "forgive me this time, and I shall never forget it: who knows but what I may be able to do you a good turn some of these days?"

The lion was so tickled at the idea of the mouse being able to help him that he lifted up his paw and let him go.

Some time after the lion was caught in a trap, and the hunters, who desired to carry him alive to the king, tied him to a tree while they went in search of a wagon to carry him on. Just then the little mouse happened to pass by, and seeing the sad plight of the lion, went up to him and soon gnawed away the ropes that bound the King of the Beasts.

"Was I not right?" said the little mouse. "Little friends may prove a great help."

Must you follow the same calling throughout your life, or might a calling change as you grow, age, and change? Is a hero's journey a singular calling or a series of meaningful adventures? Or do these meaningful adventures culminate into one grand calling?

APPLE-SEED JOHN

John Chapman (1774-1845)
Carolyn S. Bailey

There was once a farmer who had worked in the fields all his life. Every year he had ploughed and planted and harvested, and no one else had raised such fine crops as he. It seemed as if he needed to only touch the corn to have it yellow and ripen upon the ear, or lay his hand upon the rough bark of a tree to be sure that the blossoms would show and the branches hang low with fruit.

But, after years and years, the farmer grew to be an old man. His hair and beard became as white as the blossoms on the pear trees, and his back was bent and crooked, because he had worked so hard. He could only sit in the sunshine and watch someone else ploughing and planting where he wanted so much to plough and plant. And he felt very unhappy, because he wished to do something great for other people, and he was not able, for he was poor.

But one morning he got down his stout cane from the chimney corner, and he slung an empty bag over his crooked old shoulders, and he started out into the world, because he had thought of a good deed that even an old man could do.

Over the meadows and through the lanes he traveled, stopping to speak to the little wild mice, or the crickets, or the chipmunks, who knew him—all of them—and were never afraid when he went by. At every farmhouse he rested and rapped at the door and asked for—what do you think?—just a few apples! And the farmers had so many apples that they were glad to give some of them away, and the old man's bag was soon full to the very brim.

On and on he went, until he left the houses far behind, and took his way through the deep woods. At night he slept upon a bed of moss out under the stars, with the prairie dogs barking in his ears, and the owls hooting in the tops of the trees; and in the morning he started on his way again.

When he was hungry he ate of the berries that grew in the woods, but not one of his apples—oh, no! Sometimes an Indian met him, and they walked along together; and so, at last, the old man came to a place where there were wide fields, but no one to plant them, for there were no farms.

Then he sat down and took out his jack-knife, and began carefully cutting the core from every apple in his bag. With his stout cane he bored deep holes in the earth, and in every hole he dropped an apple core, to sleep there in the rain and the sun. And when his bag was emptied he hurried on to a town where he could ask for more apples.

Soon the farmers came to know him, and they called him old Apple-seed John. They gave him their very best apples for seed—the Pound Sweets, and the Sheep's Noses, and the Pippins, and the Seek-no-Farthers. They saved clippings from the pear trees, and the plum trees, and the peach trees for him; and they gave him the corner of the settle which was nearest the fire when he stopped with them for a night.

Such wonderful stories as he told the children of the things he had seen in his travels—the Indians with their gay blankets and feathers, the wolves who came out of the wood at night to look at him with their glaring eyes, the deer who ran across his path, and the shy little hares. And no one wished Apple-seed John to travel on the next morning, but he would never stay. With his bag over his shoulder, his clippings under his arm, and his trusty cane in his hand, he hurried on to plant young orchards by every river and in every lonely pasture. And soon the apple seeds that had been asleep when Apple-seed John had dropped them into the earth awoke and arose, and sent out green shoots, and began to be trees. Higher and higher they grew, until, in the wind and the sun, they covered the ground with blossoms, and then with ripe fruit, so that all the empty places in the country were full of orchards.

After a while old Apple-seed John went to live with the angels, but no one ever forgot him; and the children who knew him, when they had grown to be grandfathers themselves, would sit out under the trees, and say to each other: "This orchard was planted by Apple-seed John."

Does a calling come from outside of you, or does it come from within? Or is it often a combination of the two?

VOCATION

Frederick Buechner (1926–)

"Vocation" comes from the Latin *vocare* (to call) and means the work a man is called to by God.

There are all different kinds of voices calling you to all different kinds of work, and the problem is to find out which is the voice of God rather than of society, say, or the superego, or self-interest.

The kind of work God usually calls you to is the kind of work (a) that *you* need to do and (b) that the *world* needs to have done.

If you find your work rewarding, you have presumably met requirement (a), but if your work does not benefit others, the chances are you have missed requirement (b).

On the other hand, if your work does benefit others, you have probably met requirement (b), but if most of the time you are unhappy with it, the chances are you have not only bypassed (a) but probably aren't helping your customers much either.

Neither the hair shirt nor the soft berth will do. The place God calls you to is the place where your deep gladness and the world's deep hunger meet.

Ask This

Here are some questions to help you assess yourself and your potential:

What skills and talents do you possess?

What do you enjoy doing?

What do you love doing so much that you lose yourself in it?

What do you hate doing?

Do you tend to rush into things, or hesitate too long?

Do you tend to save up for a rainy day, or does every cent burn a hole in your pocket?

Are you a perfectionist who always demands the best, or are you satisfied with better-than-before?

Are you a natural optimist, or do you tend toward pessimism?

What do you have to offer?

What can you do that no one else can do?

What needs do you see in the world around you?

Are you willing to take risks in the hope of great rewards?

Are you ready to use your resources—your natural talents, your ideas, your money—instead of burying them?

Try This

Who do you want to become?

Sometimes it's useful to talk with people who see things from a different perspective. As you consider your life goals, it might be a good idea to visit someone elderly. Ask him or her about his/her greatest joys and greatest regrets.

Then imagine that you are very old, and a younger person has come to ask you the same questions you just asked. Write down what you would like to be able to say:

What would you like to be known for?

What would you like to have accomplished?

What sort of person would you like to have become?

These three questions are very important. They help you begin your journey with the end clearly in mind.

3

THE IMPORTANCE
OF SETTING GUARDRAILS

Movies and books are full of tales of men and women who went careening over the edge of the road and down to their destruction, who chose to "bargain with the devil" to gain their grail and discovered too late that they lost themselves in the process.

A wise man once asked, "What good will it be for a man if he gains the whole world, yet forfeits his soul?" It's a question that each of us would do well to ask, and one that invites other questions: What lines will I never cross? What cost is too high? What moral or ethical boundaries will I always observe?

Consider, as well, people you admire and respect. How did they stand firm when they might have fallen? What lines would they refuse to cross? How have they remained people of integrity?

Your answers to these questions are your ethical guardrails. These guardrails act just like guardrails on a highway; once firmly established, they protect us from danger when life is racing swiftly along, curving unexpectedly above sharp rocks and deep seas.

It's a good idea to set those guardrails now, and pay attention to them when circumstances tempt you to violate their boundaries.

A ROAD NOT TAKEN

Jeff Sandefer

At graduation from the Harvard Business School in 1986 I found myself with two choices: start my own company, armed with a strategy that I overconfidently believed was sure to succeed, or entertain an offer from the renowned consulting firm McKinsey & Company, a "golden ticket" job for MBA graduates and a chance to work with the best and brightest stars in business.

My final interview was with a young McKinsey partner named Jeff Skilling. In the end, I decided to start my own company, but Skilling and I became friends. In 1989, in a restaurant called Nick's Fish Market in downtown Houston, I was one of the first people with whom he shared his plans to build Enron.

Over the next few years I watched Skilling's meteoric success at Enron, and saw him acquire enough money and power to make the need for ethical guardrails seem old fashioned. It was a story that I feared wouldn't end well. And it didn't. By the end of 2001, Skilling had become a popular symbol of arrogance, corruption, and corporate fraud.

Jeff Skilling isn't evil or the devil incarnate, despite books and movies to the contrary. He is a human being with many good qualities who let himself become overwhelmed by hubris. And I had to admit how easy it would have been for me to make similar mistakes—mistakes that could well have led to my spending the rest of my life in a federal prison, in a cell next to the one Jeff Skilling now occupies.

After watching the rise and fall of Enron, and the corrupting influence of money and power, I started encouraging my students to make a list of "I will nots"—actions like cheating on a spouse or embezzling money—the lines that they promise never to cross, no matter the temptations.

I also encourage my students to write a "letter to self," with advice to themselves, to be opened whenever they might be tempted cross such a line, and seal it and place it in a safe place, to be opened when needed, as it surely will be. Because the more success you have, the more likely it is that the letter and ethical guardrails will be needed.

Ethical guardrails and the question "Was I a good person?" are not a quest for moral perfection. It's a fool's errand to long for Heaven on earth, with ourselves at the center. Guardrails need to be in place to serve as wake-up calls, clear signals that important lines have been crossed, and more serious mistakes loom. They are clear signals for the need to call a "time out" for some serious reflection and perhaps to repent and ask for forgiveness.

"Was I a good person?" isn't a search for perfection, but rather is asking if I have lived my life so as to become the person God intended me to be. Because anyone who can answer "yes" to this question, has lived a wonderful life indeed.

ON THE PLAYGROUND

Rev. Robert Sirico

In our grade school in Brooklyn, sports were a normal part of our day, as were schoolyard fights, cliques, and jealousies. It was on the playground, when I was about eleven years old, that I witnessed something which has stuck with me ever since.

Ellen was a classmate who immediately stood out—and not in a pleasant way. She was the same age as the rest of us, but she had matured prematurely, and on the sides of her face hair had begun to grow. It did not help that Ellen could not speak very well and slurred her words. Her classmates were, need I say, merciless.

Michael, on the other hand, was the all-around sportsman: agile, friendly, with an attractive face and welcoming smile. We all admired him, even if we would not admit it.

Poor Ellen developed a crush on Michael, which was no secret to any of us, except Michael—or so I thought.

During recess one day everyone was out on the court playing, if my memory serves, some form of dodgeball, where sides were chosen and someone from each side would throw the ball at an opponent on the opposite team. Naturally, Ellen managed to get on Michael's team to be near him.

The game started out as usual but at some point it took an ugly and energetic turn with player after player aiming directly and with full force at Ellen. With bystanders egging the players on, the viciousness of the play nudged the game toward a mob scene. Those of us on the court barely realized what we were caught up in until Michael repeatedly returned the ball in three or four rapid successions to the other team, nailing each time the ringleaders of the brawl.

I quickly recognized Michael's intentions, but it was not obvious to most of the players—he was defending Ellen's dignity without letting anyone know what he was doing. I doubt that even Ellen knew what happened.

I later came to realize that Michael knew all along that Ellen was infatuated with him. He only played at not knowing so as to avoid awkwardness.

The heroic moment, to my mind, was at precisely the instant where Michael's dark side might have taken over, when—insulated from risk by his own athleticism and popularity—he might have further enhanced his popularity by joining in with the others, at the seemingly tiny expense of letting poor despised Ellen be humiliated yet again.

But he didn't. He chose to be heroic.

Sometimes a little caution can prevent great disasters.

THE FOX AND THE GOAT

Aesop (circa 620–560 BC)

A Fox fell into a well, and though it was not very deep, he found that he could not get out again. After he had been in the well a long time, a thirsty Goat came by.

The Goat thought the Fox had gone down to drink, and so he asked if the water was good. "The finest in the whole country," said the crafty Fox, "jump in and try it. There is more than enough for both of us."

The thirsty Goat immediately jumped in and began to drink. The Fox just as quickly jumped on the Goat's back and leaped from the tip of the Goat's horns out of the well.

The foolish Goat now saw what a plight he had got into, and begged the Fox to help him out. But the Fox was already on his way to the woods.

"If you had as much sense as you have beard, old fellow," he said as he ran, "you would have been more cautious about finding a way to get out again before you jumped in."

Look before you leap.

Sometimes we don't listen to advice because we think we know best; other times we listen, but later, in the excitement of the moment, we forget.

ICARUS AND DAEDALUS *(Excerpted and Abridged)*

Ancient Greek myth as told by

Josephine Preston Peabody

Among all those mortals who grew so wise that they learned the secrets of the gods, none was more cunning than Dædalus.

He once built, for King Minos of Crete, a wonderful Labyrinth of winding ways so cunningly tangled up and twisted around that, once inside, you could never find your way out again without a magic clue.

But the king's favor veered with the wind, and one day he had his master architect imprisoned in a tower. Dædalus managed to escape from his cell; but it seemed impossible to leave the island, since every ship that came or went was well guarded by order of the king.

At length, watching the sea-gulls in the air—the only creatures that were sure of liberty—he thought of a plan for himself and his young son Icarus, who was captive with him.

Little by little, he gathered a store of feathers great and small. He fastened these together with thread, moulded them in with wax, and so fashioned two great wings like those of a bird. When they were done, Dædalus fitted them to his own shoulders, and after one or two efforts, he found that by waving his arms he could winnow the air and cleave it, as a swimmer does the sea. He held himself aloft, wavered this way and that with the wind, and at last, like a great fledgling, he learned to fly.

Without delay, he fell to work on a pair of wings for the boy Icarus, and taught him carefully how to use them, bidding him beware of rash adventures among the stars. "Remember," said the father, "never to fly very low or very high, for the fogs about the earth would weigh you down, but the blaze of the sun will surely melt your feathers apart if you go too near."

For Icarus, these cautions went in at one ear and out by the other. Who could remember to be careful when he was to fly for the first time? Are birds careful? Not they! And not an idea remained in the boy's head but the one joy of escape.

The day came, and the fair wind that was to set them free. The father bird put on his wings, and, while the light urged them to be gone, he waited to see that all was well with Icarus, for the two could not fly hand in hand. Up they rose, the boy after his father. The hateful ground of Crete sank beneath them; and the country folk, who caught a glimpse of them when they were high above the tree-tops, took it for a vision of the gods,—Apollo, perhaps, with Cupid after him.

At first there was a terror in the joy. The wide vacancy of the air dazed them,—a glance downward made their brains reel. But when a great wind filled their wings, and Icarus felt himself sustained, like a halcyon-bird in the hollow of a wave, like a child uplifted by his mother, he forgot everything in the world but joy. He forgot Crete and the other islands that he had passed over: he saw but vaguely that winged thing in the distance before him that was his father Dædalus. He longed for one draught of flight to quench the thirst of his captivity: he stretched out his arms to the sky and made towards the highest heavens.

Alas for him! Warmer and warmer grew the air. Those arms, that had seemed to uphold him, relaxed. His wings wavered, drooped. He fluttered his young hands vainly,—he was falling,—and in that terror he remembered. The heat of the sun had melted the wax from his wings; the feathers were falling, one by one, like snowflakes; and there was none to help.

He fell like a leaf tossed down the wind, down, down, with one cry that overtook Dædalus far away. When he returned, and sought high and low for the poor boy, he saw nothing but the bird-like feathers afloat on the water, and he knew that Icarus was drowned.

After leaving the underworld of Hades and arriving at the island of Ææa, the Greek hero Odysseus is warned of dangers that lie ahead in his quest to return home.

ODYSSEUS AND THE SIRENS *(Excerpted and Abridged)*

Homer *(circa 1100–850 BC)*

Retold by Josephine Preston Peabody

Odysseus came once more to Ææa. There he tarried but a little time, till Circe had told him all the dangers that beset his way. Many a good counsel and crafty warning did she give him against the Sirens that charm with their singing. So the king and his men set out from the island of Ææa.

Now very soon they came to the Sirens who sing so sweetly that they lure to death every man who listens. For straightway he is mad to be with them; and alas for the man that would fly without wings!

But when the ship drew near the Sirens' island, Odysseus did as Circe had taught him. He bade all his shipmates stop up their ears with moulded wax, so that they could not hear. He alone kept his hearing; but he had himself lashed to the mast so that he could in no wise move, and he forbade them to loose him, however he might plead, under the spell of the Sirens.

As they sailed near, his soul gave way. He heard a wild sweetness coaxing the air, as a minstrel coaxes the harp; and there, close by, were the Sirens sitting in a blooming meadow that hid the bones of men. Beautiful, winning maidens they looked; and they sang, entreating Odysseus by name to listen and abide and rest. Their voices were golden-sweet above the sound of wind and wave, like drops of amber floating on the tide; and for all his wisdom, Odysseus strained at his bonds and begged his men to let him go free. But they, deaf alike to the song and the sorcery, rowed harder than ever.

At length, song and island faded in the distance. Odysseus came to his wits once more, and his men loosed his bonds and set him free.

The psalmist prayed, "Teach us to number our days that we may get a heart of wisdom." In this vein, the poem "Ozymandias" impresses upon us our mortality and so invites a humility that may steer us around reckless pride.

OZYMANDIAS

Percy Bysshe Shelley (1792-1822)

I met a traveler from an antique land,
Who said "two vast and trunkless legs of stone
Stand in the desert … near them, on the sand,
Half sunk a shattered visage lies, whose frown,
And wrinkled lips, and sneer of cold command,
Tell that its sculptor well those passions read
Which yet survive, stamped on these lifeless things,
The hand that mocked them, and the heart that fed;
And on the pedestal these words appear:
My name is OZYMANDIAS, King of Kings,
Look on my Works ye Mighty, and despair!
Nothing beside remains. Round the decay
Of that Colossal Wreck, boundless and bare
The lone and level sands stretch far away."

The heroine in this story must decide which is more important to her: her integrity or the carrot of commendation?

THE EMPEROR OF FLOWER SEEDS
Chinese Folktale

Long ago there lived an emperor whose most precious treasure was his green thumb. Any plant he touched flourished—flowers, bushes, lovely fruit trees. This was his great gift, and in between ruling the people, he loved to work in the palace gardens, instructing the hundreds of gardeners under his command.

The people greatly admired their emperor, but as he grew old and then older still, they began to worry. The emperor had no children; who would rule over them when he was gone?

One day the emperor invited everyone in the land to his palace, as he sometimes did, to walk among his lovely gardens. As the people enjoyed the shady trees, the graceful bridges over streams of sparkling water rimmed with banks of flowers, the small pagodas where one could sit and rest in silence, the emperor walked among his people. He carried a small, red silk bag, and in that bag were flower seeds of many sizes and shapes. The emperor gave each young person one single seed, a special gift.

Then he climbed the hundred steps to the palace doors and turned to face the crowd. They grew utterly silent, so silent that the emperor did not even have to raise his voice. He said, "In six month's time, return here and show me what you have grown with the one seed I have given you."

One young woman who received a seed that day was named Lian. She lived alone with her father, who was much admired for his wisdom and honesty—though some said if he had been less honest he might have been richer, while others said less honesty would have made him poorer.

His daughter Lian was like him, and because she had a gift for growing plants, she was especially pleased with her gift seed from the emperor.

"Won't it be nice to please the emperor!" she said to her father, and she filled her favorite blue flowerpot with rich soil and planted the seed. She set it in a sunny window and watered it every day, expecting to grow a beautiful flower for the emperor.

Days passed, and while Lian's other plants flourished, nothing grew in the blue pot. Lian transferred the seed into her second-favorite pot, a yellow one, larger than the blue. Still nothing grew, and the six months passed, and it was time to return once more to the palace. How could she face the emperor with nothing?

But it would not do to stay home and ignore the emperor's instructions to return, so Lian and her father set out for the palace. On the road were many young people, all carrying pots of gorgeous flowers. Some of them laughed at her pot of dirt; others whispered and pointed at her. She saw one of her friends holding an especially flamboyant flower. "You're taking only an empty pot?" asked the friend. "I thought you were supposed to be good at gardening."

Lian's father brushed the tears from her cheeks. "You did all anyone could do, my daughter. Now hold up your head."

The grounds of the palace were filled with young men and women, all proudly displaying beautiful flowers framed with flourishing green foliage. The emperor walked among the people and bent his gray head over each flower. Lian stood at the very back of the crowd, tucked behind her father, hoping the emperor would not notice her.

But he did. He noticed her, and he spoke to her. "Why did you bring an empty pot?" he asked quietly.

"Your majesty," said Lian, bowing low. "Please accept my apologies. I was happy to receive a seed from the emperor himself. I planted that seed and tended it as best as I knew how, but nothing grew." Venturing to glance at the emperor, she saw a twinkle in his eyes that gave her courage to continue. "Because you asked us to return and show what we had grown, today I brought to you the empty pot. I am very sorry to disappoint, especially because I wished to honor as great a gardener as yourself."

To her surprise, the emperor began to smile. He beckoned for Lian to follow him to the front of the crowd, and up the hundred steps to the palace doors.

There he turned. Silence fell, and he said, "This is my successor. She will learn from me how to rule, and when I die she will be empress and rule over you, for you are not worthy of such power, and she is."

Shocked by his harsh words, Lian looked down at the crowd and saw that each young man and each young woman looked shamefaced. She was bewildered. "But, your majesty," she said quietly, so that only he could hear her, "You love plants and flowers, and all these people have brought beautiful plants to show you. All I could bring you was this pot of dirt."

"You brought exactly what I wanted," said the emperor. "The seeds I gave had been cooked. Not one of them could ever grow. Only you had the courage and honesty to appear before me bearing in your hands the truth, and truth is what every ruler and every kingdom needs and must seek."

Sometimes we are not rewarded for our integrity; sometimes we suffer for it. Why should you cling to your principles even if you will suffer for them?

SIR THOMAS MORE

Rev. Robert Sirico and Amanda Witt

Many people know about Henry VIII, the king of England who ran through six wives in his zeal to have a son. Over the course of his reign he divorced two of these wives and had two of them beheaded (another died of natural causes, and the last wife survived him).

Early on, King Henry ran into trouble because the pope refused to annul his marriage to his first wife, Katherine of Aragon; so Henry had himself named Supreme Head of the Church of England (in 1534) and annulled his marriage himself.

Then, to consolidate his power, Henry had an Act passed that required all English subjects, if asked, to take an oath affirming his supremacy over the pope (this Act was called "the Act of Succession" because it also fiddled with succession to the throne by declaring the daughter born to Henry's first wife a bastard). All of Henry's advisors were required to swear their allegiance to the Act of Succession.

One prominent advisor, Sir Thomas More—a devout Catholic—refused. Because he was an honest man who would not sell his integrity to save his life, today he is widely admired by Protestants and Catholics, believers and non-believers alike.

His reasons are beautifully portrayed in the film *A Man for All Seasons*, based on Robert Bolt's play. There More tells his daughter, "When a man takes an oath, Meg, he's holding his own self in his own hands. Like water. If he opens his fingers *then*—he needn't hope to find himself again."

Unfortunately, More was surrounded by less scrupulous men, including one named Richard Rich. More had known Rich for many years, and noting the younger man's moral instability, had urged him to choose a career path that would not place him in the way of frequent temptation, as a post in the king's court had. "Why not be a teacher?" More suggested. "You'd be a fine teacher; perhaps a great one."

Rich shrugged this off. "If I was," he said, "Who would know it?"

"You; your pupils; your friends; God," More replied. "Not a bad public, that."

More perhaps was hoping that Rich would reflect on a question that Jesus had posed to a crowd long ago: "What does it profit a man if he gains the whole world but loses his soul?" But Rich was ambitious, and in his desire for wealth and power he became increasingly unscrupulous.

Meanwhile, having refused to swear the oath affirming King Henry's religious authority, More was imprisoned in the Tower of London for a year and then brought to trial. During the trial Richard Rich brought evidence—false evidence—against his old friend.

More listened to the false evidence, then interrupted the proceedings. "I have one question to ask the witness," he said. "That's a chain of office you are wearing. May I see it?"

Rich reluctantly approached the prisoner, and More examined the medallion. "The red dragon. What's this?"

Another man explained: "Sir Richard is appointed Attorney-General for Wales."

More looked into Richard Richard's face with pain and amusement. "For Wales?" he said. "Why Richard, it profits a man nothing to give his soul for the whole world ... but for Wales?"

Richard Rich went on to become Lord Chancellor of England, wielding great power—and persecuting many honest men. He died peacefully at home in 1567.

Sir Thomas More maintained his integrity and was beheaded on July 6, 1535. His body was buried, but his head was fixed on a pike over London bridge for a month, until his daughter managed to rescue it.

The epitaph on his family tomb begins, "No famous family, but of honest stock."

If you're ever tempted to tell yourself that one small failure in integrity is no big deal, consider the following:

WHEN THE NAZIS CAME

Martin Niemöller (1892-1984)

When the Nazis came for the communists,
I remained silent;
I was not a communist.

When they locked up the social democrats,
I remained silent;
I was not a social democrat.

When they came for the trade unionists,
I did not speak out;
I was not a trade unionist.

When they came for the Jews,
I remained silent;
I wasn't a Jew.

When they came for me,
there was no one left to speak out.

Ask This

How do you decide when to take advice, and when to ignore it? What are the qualifications of a good counselor?

Some people pray for guidance. If you're one who prays, should you pray only during emergencies? Can you pray in advance? How might this be helpful?

Is there ever a good reason for ignoring your ethical guardrails?

What might tempt you, personally, to ignore your ethical guardrails? Are you overly concerned about what other people think? Are you afraid of being laughed at? Do you have a healthy competitive streak that, taken to excess, would tempt you to do whatever it takes to win?

Try This

Have you ever been tempted to rationalize, to pretend to yourself that you aren't shifting ground?

Is any human free of this temptation?

To protect yourself from yourself, write down your list of "I will never" and "I will always" guardrails. Keep this list where you can see it—on your bathroom mirror, perhaps—to remind yourself to be absolutely honest with yourself.

4

WHAT COMPANIONS
DO YOU WANT WITH YOU
ON YOUR JOURNEY?

W hat sort of companions will you need on your hero's journey? To answer this question you must consider your own strengths and weaknesses.

Seeking out friends who are strong where we are weak doesn't always come naturally. Sometimes we even feel defensive around people who are better than we are in certain areas, and we become unnecessarily competitive or envious of them.

It takes humility to admit that others are better than we are at certain things, and that these other things are important. This sort of honesty is hard, but it is the stuff of real humility (quite distinct from being a wimp) and will bring us indispensible and highly beneficial companions for our journey.

Humility, of course, is only a start. Strong, loyal relationships also require effort. Set aside time for those who have always supported you; show them that you will always support them. Be curious about other people's hopes and dreams; learn to be interested; seek ways to help. You might be surprised to find that as you focus on someone other than yourself, your own problems shrink; your horizons open up; your perspective broadens and deepens. Eventually you will find yourself part of a healthy support network, a community that will help sustain you through your hero's journey even as you sustain others through theirs.

Much of our long-term happiness comes from strong, relationships, but such relationships require a deliberate investment of time and thought. As you sow, so shall you reap.

THE GARDEN

Rev. Robert Sirico

Over the course of several years when I was upgrading my fluency in Italian, I would go with some seminarians to the small northern Italian town of Verbania located on Lago Maggiore, not very far from Switzerland and the Italian Alps. There I would spend the better part of two weeks in the company of any number of Italian high school teachers who had the summer job of tutoring non-Italian students in their language.

The setting was idyllic: an old monastery had been turned into a "pensione"—a kind of economical hotel. There I spend many pleasant hours reading Machiavelli or Mansone in the original; writing a speech I might have to give in Italian and having it corrected by my tutor; trying to grasp the meaning of some Italian idiom (which still elude me).

One day in the garden of the monastery, where I was reading, I noticed two elderly ladies making their way through the flowers, negotiating the unsteady cobblestoned path, pausing from time to time over this or that flower or cluster of greenery.

As I watched them I realized something amazing which I might have missed if there were distractions: One of the ladies was rather badly crippled, and while she was able to walk, it would have been very perilous on the unsure footing of the garden. The other woman was a bit younger, and steady on her feet; but she was blind.

Together, they experience a lovely Italian garden that neither could have negotiated alone.

CHOOSE YOUR FELLOW TRAVELERS WELL

Jeff Sandefer

One of my biggest failings is that I have not been particular enough about those I choose as companions on the journey (and I'm sure many have felt the same about me!).

The temptation in launching a business is to "get started now," no matter what the costs. That means accepting some team members, customers, or suppliers who don't have the requisite passion, skill, or integrity, just to fill a need. This is always—and I mean always—a mistake.

The temptation with family and friends is to tolerate people who tear us down instead of building us up, or who tell us pleasant lies instead of bitter truths. Too often we take the easy way out to avoid conflict. But sticking our heads into the sand makes us less than we should be.

Don't get me wrong. I've been blessed with some of the finest friends, investors, customers, partners, and employees in the world—people who have performed extraordinary acts of kindness and generosity and who have treated me with far more loyalty and forbearance than I deserve.

But often I have been in too much of a hurry, and that has delayed me in my quests. I've been determined to "make it happen" and willing to settle for "good enough" in people, work ethic, talent, and character.

So I pray you'll learn from my mistakes:

Lesson One: Surround yourself with people of integrity. We all have lapses, but it's pretty easy to tell the difference between people who are trying to be good and people who aren't. And yes—people can change. But it's a terrible bet to believe that they will. So surround yourself with people who strive to make ethical choices, who don't cut corners, who are unflinchingly honest with themselves and with you.

Lesson Two: Surround yourself with people who are optimistic and kind. Life is just too short to surround yourself with jerks.

Lesson Three: Surround yourself with people who are passionate. A high IQ and raw talent are no substitute for integrity and passion. Choose companions who are pursuing a "calling." Don't tolerate those who are just "phoning it in"—they will be far happier somewhere else and inevitably become a soul killing cancer for the group.

And never forget that your spouse is your most significant companion of all. Especially mine.

Do your friends complement you, or merely compliment you? In other words, are you willing to surround yourself with people who possess strengths that you yourself lack, or do you just surround yourself with people whose words or weaknesses flatter you?

THE WONDERFUL WIZARD OF OZ *(Excerpted)*

L. Frank Baum (1856-1919)

They walked along listening to the singing of the brightly colored birds and looking at the lovely flowers which now became so thick that the ground was carpeted with them. There were big yellow and white and blue and purple blossoms, besides great clusters of scarlet poppies, which were so brilliant in color they almost dazzled Dorothy's eyes.

"Aren't they beautiful?" the girl asked, as she breathed in the spicy scent of the bright flowers.

"I suppose so," answered the Scarecrow. "When I have brains, I shall probably like them better."

"If I only had a heart, I should love them," added the Tin Woodman.

"I always did like flowers," said the Lion. "They seem so helpless and frail. But there are none in the forest so bright as these."

They now came upon more and more of the big scarlet poppies, and fewer and fewer of the other flowers; and soon they found themselves in the midst of a great meadow of poppies. Now it is well known that when there are many of these flowers together their odor is so powerful that anyone who breathes it falls asleep, and if the sleeper is not carried away from the scent of the flowers, he sleeps on and on forever. But Dorothy did not know this, nor could she get away from the bright red flowers that were everywhere about; so presently her eyes grew heavy and she felt she must sit down to rest and to sleep.

But the Tin Woodman would not let her do this.

"We must hurry and get back to the road of yellow brick before dark," he said; and the Scarecrow agreed with him. So they kept walking until Dorothy could stand no longer. Her eyes closed in spite of herself and she forgot where she was and fell among the poppies, fast asleep.

"What shall we do?" asked the Tin Woodman.

"If we leave her here she will die," said the Lion. "The smell of the flowers is killing us all. I myself can scarcely keep my eyes open, and the dog is asleep already."

It was true; Toto had fallen down beside his little mistress. But the Scarecrow and the Tin Woodman, not being made of flesh, were not troubled by the scent of the flowers.

"Run fast," said the Scarecrow to the Lion, "and get out of this deadly flower bed as soon as you can. We will bring the little girl with us, but if you should fall asleep you are too big to be carried."

So the Lion aroused himself and bounded forward as fast as he could go. In a moment he was out of sight.

"Let us make a chair with our hands and carry her," said the Scarecrow. So they picked up Toto and put the dog in Dorothy's lap, and then they made a chair with their hands for the seat and their arms for the arms and carried the sleeping girl between them through the flowers.

On and on they walked, and it seemed that the great carpet of deadly flowers that surrounded them would never end....

They carried the sleeping girl to a pretty spot beside the river, far enough from the poppy field to prevent her breathing any more of the poison of the flowers, and here they laid her gently on the soft grass and waited for the fresh breeze to waken her.

There is the sort of friend who is full of enthusiasm, but disappears when the going gets tough. Do you have friends who will stay with you and help you when the going gets rough?

THE PILGRIM'S PROGRESS *(Excerpted and Abridged)*

John Bunyan (1628-1688)

Language modernized by Mary Macgregor

[*The hero of the story, named Christian, wants to reach the wicket gate and so enter on the path toward the blessed country. As he walks, he tells his companion, Pliable, about all the wonders of this far country to which they are headed.*]

As Pliable heard of the excellence of the country and of the company to which they were going, he said, "Well, my good companion, glad am I to hear of these things. Come on, let us go with more speed."

"I cannot go as fast as I would by reason of this burden that is on my back," said Christian.

Now I saw in my dream that just as they had ended their talk, they drew nigh to a bog that was in the midst of the plain, and they being heedless did both fall suddenly into it. The name of this bog was the Slough of Despond.

Here therefore they struggled for a time, being grievously covered with dirt. And Christian, because of the burden that was on his back, began to sink in the mire.

Then said Pliable, "Ah, Neighbour Christian, where are you now?"

"Truly," said Christian, "I do not know."

At this Pliable began to be offended, and said angrily, "Is this the happiness you have told me of all this while? If I get out again with my life, you shall possess the wonderful country alone."

And with that he gave a desperate struggle or two, and got out of the mire on that side of the bog which was next to his own house. So away he went, and Christian saw him no more.

Christian was left to tumble in the Slough of Despond alone. But still he tried to struggle to that side of the Slough that was further from his own house, and next to the Wicket-gate. But he could not get out because of the burden that was upon his back.

And I beheld in my dream that a man came to him, whose name was Help, and asked him what he did there.

"Sir," said Christian, "I was bid to go this, and as I was going thither I fell in here."

"Why did you not look for the steps?" said Help.

"I was so full of fear," answered Christian, "that I fled the next way and fell in."

Then said Help, "Give me thy hand." So Christian gave him his hand, and he drew him out and set him upon sound ground, and bid him go on his way.

When a fair weather friend shows his true colors, do you ignore the signs or heed them?

THE TRAVELERS AND THE BEAR

Aesop (circa 620–560 BC)

Two friends were walking along the road, when a Bear came suddenly upon them. One of them got first to a tree, and climbed up into it and hid among the branches.

The other, who was slower, fell flat upon the ground, and made believe that he was dead.

When the Bear came up to him, and poked him with his nose, he held his breath; for it is said that this animal will not touch a dead man.

The Bear went off, and the Man who was in the tree came down, and asked the other what the Bear had whispered.

"He told me," said the other, "not to travel with friends who would desert me when danger came."

Are you and your companions able to set aside minor differences in order to work together toward a common goal?

The Farmer and His Sons

Aesop (circa 620-560 BC)

Retold by James Baldwin

A farmer had seven sons, who could never agree among themselves. He had often told them how foolish they were to be always quarreling, but they kept on and paid no heed to his words.

One day he called them before him, and showed them a bundle of seven sticks tied tightly together. "See which one of you can break that bundle," he said.

Each one took the bundle in his hands, and tried his best to break it; but it was so strong that they could not even bend it. At last they gave it back to their father, and said:

"We cannot break it."

Then he untied the bundle, and gave a single stick to each of his sons.

"Now see what you can do," he said. Each one broke his stick with great ease.

"My sons," said the Farmer, "you, like these sticks, will be strong if you will stand together, but weak while each is for himself."

Ecclesiastes 4:9-12

King James Version

Two *are* better than one; because they have a good reward for their labour. For if they fall, the one will lift up his fellow: but woe to him *that is* alone when he falleth; for *he hath* not another to help him up. Again, if two lie together, then they have heat: but how can one be warm *alone*? And if one prevail against him, two shall withstand him; and a threefold cord is not quickly broken.

It's good to be a hard worker; but sometimes by ignoring the resources our companions offer, we cause ourselves more work than is necessary.

THE LEVER

Modern Folktale

A boy was earning some extra cash one hot summer day by removing rocks from the family's front yard. He moved small ones and he moved medium sized ones, and finally tackled the biggest one.

From the porch his grandfather, resting from his own labors, stood watching. The boy pulled at the rock; he pushed at the rock; he fetched a shovel and dug around the rock, exposing its deep base, and then he pushed again. Still the rock would not budge.

The grandfather sat down on the porch swing.

The boy wiped sweat from his eyes. He turned his back to the rock and leaned hard against it, shoving with all his weight. The rock did not move.

The boy pulled the garden hose over to the rock and wet the dirt at the rock's base. He took the shovel and dug beneath the rock's edges. Then he sat down on the ground and planted his feet against the rock, pushing until his face turned red.

Still the grandfather watched.

The boy turned around and sat in the mud with his back to the rock. Bracing his feet against the ground, he pushed backwards with all his might. The rock did not move.

Exhausted and filthy, the boy threw up his hands. "It won't budge," he told his grandfather. "I've tried everything. I give up."

His grandfather shook his head. "Don't give up until you've tried everything," he said.

"I *have* tried everything. Weren't you sitting there watching? I tried everything *twice!*"

"You haven't tried everything yet," the grandfather said. "You haven't tried asking my advice."

Ask This

Do I have companions who will help "keep me awake" on the journey?
Where is my most dangerous blind spot?

What has kept me from overcoming this weakness? How can I overcome it or compensate for it?

How can I enlist the aid of someone who is strong in areas where I am weak?

Can I ask someone to keep me accountable with regard to a specific danger?

I need faithful companions who help me on my journey. Am I such a companion to others?

How can I protect and nurture the relationships I already have?

Try This

Imagine some life-threatening scenario—bankruptcy, cancer, divorce, a permanent injury that destroys your career. Who would continue to stand by you? Who is most likely to run? How can you find and nurture better companions for your journey?

Often the most loyal friends are ones who feel accountable to a higher power. Consider joining a fellowship of such people. If you already belong to such a group, ask yourself how you could strengthen your ties with them.

5

STONES IN THE ROAD

On your hero's journey, when faced with one obstacle after another, exhausting day after exhausting day, what will you do?

You can feel sorry for yourself and quit. You can choose to believe the world is out to get you. You can decide that you're too weak or ignoble to succeed, that triumph is for other people. Or you can choose to see problems as opportunities, as challenges spurring new ways of thinking and personal growth.

Just as climbing mountains or pushing against weights builds strength, so climbing over or pushing against the obstacles on your hero's journey will help to build mental, emotional, and spiritual muscle. As the letter of Paul to the Romans says, "Suffering produces endurance, and endurance produces character, and character produces hope."

Your goal is important, but it is how you reach your goal, what you do before the end, that has the potential to transform your very self, so that at the end of your journey you not only achieve something great but also become something great.

Learn to work hard. Learn to endure.

THREE KINDS OF STUDENTS

Jeff Sandefer

My parents divorced when I was nine years old, and I never again lived with my mother. I was a very lonely child.

When I was twenty-seven the fate of our new company hung in the balance as I drilled my first oil well. The well came up dry.

I endured my own terrible divorce at age thirty-seven, and I feared I wouldn't be able to protect my six-month-old daughter.

Facing difficult challenges like these can be disheartening, especially after you've battled long and hard with no progress. And if it means a total loss of control, it's even more devastating to the entrepreneurial ego and identity.

Yet, it is moments like these that hone the gifts and build the character that will pave the way to future success. Sure, sometimes scars—even open wounds—remain. But if you can muster the drive, courage, and confidence to get back up and try again, you will not be defined by obstacles; you'll be defined as one who overcomes them.

As a teacher, I've seen three types of students:

The first are those who have a deep-seated anger against an authority figure—a parent, coach, or teacher, for example—who've done them some injustice. When properly guided, these types often will use their conflict to change the world for the better.

The second are those who have overcome a potentially crushing challenge: a deadly disease, the loss of a parent or sibling at an early age, extreme poverty, and the like. Typically these types have little fear, and so the trial-and-error experiments so crucial to the heroic journey feel more like adventures than ordeals. They experience each day—each minute even—as a blessing. These types attract other upbeat companions and role models and often go on to great accomplishments.

The final type seems most successful in schools and early life. They are the straight-A students who conformed to their parents' and teachers' demands, the team captains for whom athletics came easily, the popular kids. These people have never experienced failure or conflict—often because, when real life reared its head, a well-meaning parent came dashing to rescue them before they scraped a knee or received a well-deserved failing grade.

I pity this last group, because I have never had success in reaching one of them. Not a single one. Having faced no epic battles or catastrophic mistakes, they haven't learned that the sting of failure almost always is more imagined than real. To them, image matters more than reality—often, quite literally, more than life itself. Even a single failure feels as if it might cause the whole façade to come tumbling down, so risk and the genuine accomplishment that comes from taking chances are avoided at all cost.

That's why I encourage students to fail early, often, and as cheaply as possible.

No sane person welcomes stones in the road. But don't build your life around never facing one. These obstacles are the necessary means for developing the faith and persistence to overcome the real challenges that inevitably confront any person who has set out to do something heroic.

THE PERSISTENT INNOVATOR

Rev. Robert Sirico

I once spoke at the commencement of Trinity School at Meadow View, a truly impressive private high school in Falls Church, Virginia, and heard the valedictory address given by the graduating senior Beau Lovdahl, who was on his way to Princeton.

Beau told the story of Nikola Tesla, a Serbian electrical engineer who arrived in New York City in June of 1884 with a letter of recommendation to Thomas Edison from his former boss. The letter said, "I know two great men and you are one of them; the other is this young man."

What happened next is disputed. Tesla claimed that Edison offered him $50,000 dollars to redesign the company's inefficient direct current generators, and indeed Tesla promptly redesigned those generators. But when he asked Edison for his bonus, Edison merely said, "Tesla, you don't understand our American humor."

So Telsa resigned. He dug ditches to make ends meet while he planned a new system of power distribution based on alternating current—a system for which he couldn't find investors. Finally George Westinghouse hired Tesla, and in 1893 Tesla's alternating-current method won the competition to power the Chicago World's Fair. Tesla's method is used to this day to light homes and businesses around the world.

Telsa could have become the world's first billionaire, but he didn't. Why not? When Westinghouse faced a smear campaign from Edison Machine Works, Telsa tore up his royalty contract with Westinghouse in order to keep the company afloat.

Telsa went on to explore more avenues of invention, and to face more obstacles—disputed patents, quarrels over whether he deserved the Nobel Prize, problem after problem after problem. He received no credit for many of the scientific advances he pioneered, and became so peculiar that people began to avoid him, thinking him insane. He died at age eighty-six in a hotel, with little money to his name.

Here is the way Beau Lovdahl ends the tale:

> This was an ignominious end to such a remarkable life. Yet by no means should we consider his life a tragedy. Tesla's legacy was tremendous. All electricity from power plants today is generated and brought

to us by Tesla's innovations. After his death, the Supreme Court upheld Tesla as the true inventor of radio. He invented the spark plug device in car engines, and Tesla's work in the wireless transmission of power brought us inventions such as the Tesla coil, which is used today to generate artificial lightning, and tuned circuits which form the basis of wireless communications today.

He exemplified the indomitable nature of the human spirit.... Tesla pursued his ideas and interests tirelessly despite being criticized or forgotten.

Telsa was eccentric; he might well have been difficult to get along with; he might not always have been in the right. But his is a resounding model of perseverance in the face of obstacles. He pursued his dreams, his ideas, even when doing so was hard, draining, and even demeaning.

And as I sat in that auditorium watching young people preparing to strike out into the world, I was greatly encouraged to hear one of them holding up someone like Telsa as an example of what the world needs and what they themselves could become. We need brilliant men and women like Telsa: we need people with a broad vision of what can be and what really is of lasting value, people with the strength to surmount obstacles and maintain a definition of success that is deeper and more authentic than what we find in today's celebrity tabloids.

Are you ready to embrace hard work?

THE FARMER'S SONS

Aesop (circa 620–560 BC)

A rich old farmer, who felt that he had not many more days to live, called his sons to his bedside.

"My sons," he said, "heed what I have to say to you. Do not on any account part with the estate that has belonged to our family for so many generations. Somewhere on it is hidden a rich treasure. I do not know the exact spot, but it is there, and you will surely find it. Spare no energy and leave no spot unturned in your search."

The father died, and no sooner was he in his grave than the sons set to work digging with all their might, turning up every foot of ground with their spades, and going over the whole farm two or three times.

No hidden gold did they find; but at harvest time when they had settled their accounts and had pocketed a rich profit far greater than that of any of their neighbors, they understood that the treasure their father had told them about was the wealth of a bountiful crop, and that in their industry had they found the treasure.

Industry is itself a treasure.

Is a life of ease your goal? Or do you long for something that can only be attained through hard work?

THE STRENUOUS LIFE *(Excerpted)*

Theodore Roosevelt (1858-1919)

... I wish to preach, not the doctrine of ignoble ease, but the doctrine of the strenuous life, the life of toil and effort, of labor and strife; to preach that highest form of success which comes, not to the man who desires mere easy peace, but to the man who does not shrink from danger, from hardship, or from bitter toil, and who out of these wins the splendid ultimate triumph.

A life of slothful ease, a life of that peace which springs merely from lack either of desire or of power to strive after great things, is as little worthy of a nation as of an individual.... We do not admire the man of timid peace. We admire the man who embodies victorious effort; the man who never wrongs his neighbor, who is prompt to help a friend, but who has those virile qualities necessary to win in the stern strife of actual life. It is hard to fail, but it is worse to never have tried to succeed.

In this life we get nothing save by effort. Freedom from effort in the present merely means that there has been some stored up effort in the past.

... A mere life of ease is not in the end a very satisfactory life, and, above all, it is a life which ultimately unfits those who follow it for serious work in the world.... Let us therefore boldly face the life of strife, resolute to do our duty well and manfully; resolute to be both honest and brave, to serve high ideals, yet to use practical methods.

Above all, let us shrink from no strife, through hard and dangerous endeavor, that we shall ultimately win the goal of true national greatness.

The person who is willing to work hard often reaps unexpected rewards.
Do you embrace challenges?

THE STONE IN THE ROAD

Sarah Arnold (1859-1943)

There was once a very rich man who lived in a beautiful castle near a village. He loved the people who lived in the village, and he tried to help them. He planted beautiful trees near their houses, and made picnics for their children, and every Christmas he gave them a Christmas tree.

But the people did not love to work. They were very unhappy, because they, too, could not be rich—like their friend in the castle.

One day the rich man got up very early in the morning, and placed a large stone in the road which led past his house. Then he hid himself behind the hedge and waited to see what would happen.

By and by, a poor man came along driving a cow. He scolded because the stone lay in his path, but he walked around it, and went on his way. Then a farmer came, on his way to the mill. He complained, too, because the stone was there; but he, too, drove around it, and went on his way.

So the day passed. Everyone who came by scolded because the stone lay in the road, but no one touched it.

At last, just at nightfall, the miller's boy came past. He was a hard-working fellow, and was very tired, because he had been busy since early morning at the mill. But he said to himself: "It is almost dark. Somebody may fall over this stone in the night, and perhaps be badly hurt. I will move it out of the way."

So he tugged at the heavy stone. It was hard to move, but he pulled, and pushed, and lifted until at last he moved it from its place. To his surprise he found a bag lying underneath.

He lifted the bag. It was heavy, for it was filled with gold. Upon it was written: "This gold belongs to the one who moves the stone!"

The miller's boy went home with a happy heart, and the rich man went back to his castle. He was glad, indeed, that he had found someone who was not afraid to do hard things.

When faced with problems, are you willing to try, try again?

THE CROW AND THE PITCHER

Aesop (circa 620-560 BC)

A crow that was dying of thirst found a Pitcher with some water in it, but it was so low he could not reach it with his bill, although he stood on the very tips of his toes.

He tried to break the Pitcher, but it was too strong.

He tried to push it over, but it was too heavy.

At last he thought of a way; so he took a pebble and dropped it into the Pitcher, then another, and another, and, by and by, he had raised the water in the Pitcher and was able to quench his thirst.

Where there's a will there's a way.

Have you made up your mind to keep on keeping on?

EXCERPTS FROM THREE SPEECHES GIVEN DURING WORLD WAR II

Winston Churchill (1874–1965)

May 13, 1940–First Speech as Prime Minister

I would say to the House, as I said to those who have joined this government: "I have nothing to offer but blood, toil, tears and sweat."

We have before us an ordeal of the most grievous kind. We have before us many, many long months of struggle and of suffering.

You ask, what is our policy? I can say: It is to wage war, by sea, land and air, with all our might and with all the strength that God can give us; to wage war against a monstrous tyranny, never surpassed in the dark, lamentable catalogue of human crime. That is our policy.

You ask, what is our aim? I can answer in one word: It is victory, victory at all costs, victory in spite of all terror, victory, however long and hard the road may be.

June 4, 1940–Speech to the House of Commons

The British Empire and the French Republic, linked together in their cause and in their need, will defend to the death their native soil, aiding each other like good comrades to the utmost of their strength.

Even though large tracts of Europe and many old and famous States have fallen or may fall into the grip of the Gestapo and all the odious apparatus of Nazi rule, we shall not flag or fail.

We shall go on to the end, we shall fight in France, we shall fight on the seas and oceans, we shall fight with growing confidence and growing strength in the air, we shall defend our Island, whatever the cost may be, we shall fight on the beaches, we shall fight on the landing grounds, we shall fight in the fields and in the streets, we shall fight in the hills; we shall never surrender, and even if, which I do not for a moment believe, this Island or a large part of it were subjugated and starving, then our Empire beyond the seas, armed and guarded by the British Fleet, would carry on the struggle, until, in God's good time, the New World, with all its power and might, steps forth to the rescue and the liberation of the old.

October 29, 1941—Speech at a School

When I was here last time we were quite alone, desperately alone, and we had been so for five or six months. We were poorly armed. We are not so poorly armed today; but then we were very poorly armed. We had the unmeasured menace of the enemy and their air attack still beating upon us, and you yourselves had had experience of this attack; and I expect you are beginning to feel impatient that there has been this long lull with nothing particular turning up! But we must learn to be equally good at what is short and sharp and what is long and tough.

... You cannot tell from appearances how things will go. Sometimes imagination makes things out far worse than they are; yet without imagination not much can be done. Those people who are imaginative see many more dangers than perhaps exist; certainly many more than will happen; but then they must also pray to be given that extra courage to carry this far-reaching imagination.

But for everyone ... surely from this period of ten months, this is the lesson: Never give in. Never give in. Never, never, never, never—in nothing, great or small, large or petty—never give in, except to convictions of honor and good sense. Never yield to force. Never yield to the apparently overwhelming might of the enemy.

... Do not let us speak of darker days: let us speak rather of sterner days. These are not dark days; these are great days—the greatest days our country has ever lived; and we must all thank God that we have been allowed, each of us according to our stations, to play a part in making these days memorable in the history of our race.

Ask This

What do you gain from working—that is, what is the inherent value of work itself?

What is the value of the journey, separate from the destination?

Who in your life has given you a good example of endurance?

Who in your life has been a good example of a hard worker?

How can you decide when to press on against a certain obstacle, and when to go around it?

What have you successfully done that tasted sweeter because it cost you so much?

Try This

Ask ten people whether, if they won the lottery, they would quit work and live lives of leisure.

Ask the ones who say that they would keep working, why? What would they gain from working, if money were no longer an issue?

6

THE GIANT OF DESPAIR

Inevitably your hero's journey will take you into dark valleys; and as any child will tell you, failing light makes even ordinary things look dangerous. A rocking chair becomes a lurking monster; a shirt crumpled on the floor becomes a creeping octopus. Add to this a real threat—a powerful enemy or a run of bad fortune—and soon you may find yourself mired in despair.

In such a valley, when even the marked path can be missed, how does the hero maintain hope and find his way back to the light?

One thing to do is to call to mind your goal. Focus on your purpose, not on the present darkness. Remember your dream. In this your companions can help, since chances are not everyone in your life will feel discouraged at the same time.

Second, many have found that a connection to the transcendent puts temporary problems in their proper perspective. If you believe in God, then devote yourself to prayer. Ask for his help. Make a conscious effort to examine this stage of your journey in light of the broader picture.

And perhaps most fundamentally, when you are in the valley of darkness, go on believing in the light. One thinks of the Jew in Cologne, Germany who is said to have inscribed these words on a cellar wall during the Nazi Holocaust: "I believe in the sun even when it is not shining, I believe in love even when I do not feel it, I believe in God even when He is silent."

Such strategies can help you through the inevitable times of discouragement until the sunlight again returns.

ARCHBISHOP VAN THUAN

Rev. Robert Sirico

I first met the small, gentle Vietnamese priest in the outskirts of Rome when he was serving as chaplain to a convent of nuns. I had only heard bits and pieces about his life prior to our first encounter, but then, slowly, began to realize that I was in the presence of a spiritual giant.

The somewhat frail man who stood before me in a nondescript reception room in the convent was the nephew of South Vietnam's first President, Ngô Đình Diệm (an anti-Communist leader who was assassinated) and had been made an archbishop.

But not just any archbishop: he was made Archbishop of Saigon by Pope Paul VI just prior to the Communist takeover of the capitol city. As the last of the American personnel were frantically boarding helicopters with their belonging and what Vietnamese staff they could crowd aboard, the newly minted Archbishop Francis Xavier Nugen VanThuan was settling in to his episcopal residence.

Once the dust had settled and the Communists were firmly in control, they took inventory of who was in the city and discovered that Archbishop Van Thuan had arrived in Saigon shortly before the American pullout. Suspecting that the nephew of Diem was a CIA spy, they ordered him back to his home diocese of Huế.

Van Thuan replied he was no longer the bishop there, that the pope had appointed another bishop in his place, and that he was the new archbishop of Saigon.

The Communists gave him a choice: return to the North or go to jail. In obedience to his vows to the pope, Van Thuan chose jail, which turned out to be thirteen years, nine of which were in solitary confinement.

His heroic story is recounted in his own journals and in a biography published posthumously (he died of cancer in 2002, after being made a Cardinal in 2001 by Blessed John Paul II). But when I met him, none of the notoriety accompanied him. He was just a simple priest with whom I was personally getting acquainted in a simple room.

I tell this immensely inspiring and heroic story to relate one brief conversation we had. We were enjoying a Vietnamese dinner in his residence in Rome, and Van Thuan pointed to some handwritten journals on a bookshelf in the dining room.

"Those were the journals I would attempt to keep while in prison," he said.

I asked if I might look at them, and he nodded yes.

Carefully I held a tattered volume in my hands, paging through it. I noticed the journals were written in either Italian or Latin. I asked him why.

"Of course the guards could read Vietnamese and many could French," he said. "But few could read Italian and fewer still Latin. I told them they were exercise books to keep up the languages. That is why I still have them."

In those books there is a passage written early in his imprisonment that speaks of deep despair and despondency. It was difficult for me to believe that this heroic and hopeful person could have been the same one who wrote those words.

I asked about those passages and he shook his head, remembering the day he made the entry.

"The entire world was falling down around me," he said. "My family and friends, my home, my diocese and freedom had all been taken from me. And I asked God how I could do his work in this place. It seemed so dark ..."

"Did God answer?" I asked.

"Yes, eventually. He said: *Just do my will. That is the work I want you to accomplish.* And I never despaired again."

WHO WOULD CHOOSE DESPAIR?

Jeff Sandefer

Most natural entrepreneurs rise to challenges. The "stone in the road" is part of a game to be won, a chance to show what talent, hard work, and persistence can overcome. Even the fear of not making payroll can be seen as a great motivator.

But some stones are bigger than others.

My wife's parents had worked hard all of their lives, her father Mike as a minister and her mother Joanna as a minister's wife, science teacher, and full-time mother to four precocious girls. Now after thirty years, it was time to retire, to relax and travel the world.

Then suddenly a cancer from long ago returned with a vengeance. My mother-in-law had less than a week to live.

During those next few days, I had the great honor of watching Joanna die. At times she was angry; we all knew she was leaving too soon. Other times she was sad, sad to be leaving those she loved so much. But even in her most difficult moments, she was joyous too, excited that she soon would be meeting her Savior.

Joanna faced that largest stone, the stone each of us will face eventually, with dignity and without despair. Because she was certain of Who was on the other side.

Say what you want about religion and religious people, but don't underestimate the power of a transcendent Faith.

There, as I watched Joanna die, I made an important decision: I want to die like that.

Of all the gifts she gave so many people, I felt Joanna had saved the greatest gift for me. Ever since then, even the largest stones, with the right perspective, eventually seem like pebbles.

Have you ever been so discouraged that you overlooked an obvious answer to your problem?

THE PILGRIM'S PROGRESS *(Excerpted)*

John Bunyan *(1628-1688)*

Language modernized by Mary MacGregor

Said Hopeful, "Where are we now?" But Christian was silent, for he began to be afraid that he had led Hopeful out of the way.

Now it began to rain and thunder and lightning in a very dreadful manner, and the river flowed over the banks. And Hopeful groaned, "Oh that I had kept on my way."

By this time the waters were greatly risen, so that to go back was very dangerous. Yet they tried to go back, but it was so dark, and the flood was so high, that as they went they were nearly drowned nine or ten times, and they could not reach the stile again that night.

Wherefore at last, coming to a little shelter, they sat down, but being weary they fell asleep.

Now there was, not far from the place where they lay, a castle, called Doubting Castle, and the owner of the castle was Giant Despair, and it was in his grounds the pilgrims were now sleeping. Wherefore the giant, getting up early, and walking up and down in his fields, caught Christian and Hopeful asleep.

Then with a grim and surly voice he woke them, and asked them what they were doing in his grounds. They told him they were pilgrims and had lost their way.

The giant said, "You have trampled on my ground, and slept on it, and therefore you must go along with me." So they were forced to go, because he was stronger than they. Also they said very little, for they knew they had done wrong.

The giant therefore drove them before him, and put them into his castle, into a very dark dungeon. Here, then, they lay, from Wednesday morning till Saturday night, without one bit of bread or drop of drink, or light, or any one to speak to them.

Now Giant Despair had a wife, and he told her he had taken a couple of men prisoners, because they were sleeping on his grounds. Then she

81

told him that, when he arose in the morning, he should beat them without mercy. So Giant Despair got a cudgel, and went down to the dungeon and beat Christian and Hopeful fearfully, so that they could not move. Then the giant left them, and they spent their time in sighs and bitter tears.

The next night Giant Despair again talked to his wife, and she said, "Tell your prisoners to kill themselves, for they will never escape from the dungeon."

So when morning came, the giant went to them in a surly manner, and seeing they still ached with the stripes he had given them, he told them to poison themselves, for they would never get away from him in any other way. But they asked the giant to let them go.

That made him so angry that he rushed on them and would have killed them, but he fell into a fit and lost for a time the use of his hand, wherefore he withdrew and left them as before.

Well, towards evening the giant went down again to the dungeon to see if his prisoners had followed his advice and poisoned themselves. He found them alive, but because of their wounds and for want of bread and water they could do little but breathe.

Now at night the giant's wife said: "Take the prisoners into the castle yard tomorrow, and show them the bones and skulls of those prisoners you have already killed. Tell them that in a week you will tear them to pieces, as you have torn your other prisoners."

When the morning was come, the giant went to them again and took them into the castle yard, and showed them all his wife had bidden him.

"These," said he, "were pilgrims once as you are, but they walked in my grounds as you have done. And when I thought fit, I tore them in pieces, and so within ten days I will do to you. Get you down to your den again," and he beat them all the way there.

That night, about midnight, Christian and Hopeful began to pray, and they prayed till dawn of day.

Now just at dawn Christian spoke in sudden amazement. "How foolish we are to lie here, when we might be free after all. I have a key in my pocket called Promise, that will, I am persuaded, open any lock in Doubting Castle."

Then said Hopeful, "That is good news, pull it out of your pocket and try."

Christian pulled it out and began to try the dungeon door, and the bolt, as he turned the key, yielded, and the door flew open, and Christian and Hopeful both came out. Then he went to the door that led to the castle yard, and with his key opened that door also, after that he went to the iron gate, for that must be opened too. That lock was terribly hard, yet the key did open it.

Then they thrust open the gate to make their escape in haste, but, as it opened, that gate made such a creaking that it waked Giant Despair, who got up hastily to follow his prisoners, but he could not run after them, for again he took one of his fits.

Then Christian and Hopeful went on till they came to the King's highway and so were safe, because they were out of the giant's grounds.

Now when they had got over the stile, they began to wonder what they should do to keep other pilgrims from falling into the hands of Giant Despair. So they agreed to put up there a pillar, and to write on it this sentence: "Over this stile is the way to Doubting Castle, which is kept by Giant Despair, who despiseth the King of the Celestial Country and seeks to destroy His holy pilgrims."

Many pilgrims, that came after, read what was written and escaped Giant Despair.

When the present situation is grim, how can you reflect on your dreams, your goal, in a way that will inspire you to press on?

I HAVE A DREAM *(Excerpted)*

Martin Luther King, Jr. (1929-1968)

Let us not wallow in the valley of despair. I say to you today, my friends, that even though we face the difficulties of today and tomorrow, I still have a dream. It is a dream deeply rooted in the American dream.

I have a dream that one day this nation will rise up and live out the true meaning of its creed: "We hold these truths to be self-evident: that all men are created equal."

I have a dream that one day on the red hills of Georgia the sons of former slaves and the sons of former slave owners will be able to sit down together at the table of brotherhood.

I have a dream that one day even the state of Mississippi, a state sweltering with the heat of injustice, sweltering with the heat of oppression, will be transformed into an oasis of freedom and justice.

I have a dream that my four little children will one day live in a nation where they will not be judged by the color of their skin but by the content of their character.

I have a dream today.

I have a dream that one day, down in Alabama, with its vicious racists … one day right there in Alabama, little black boys and black girls will be able to join hands with little white boys and white girls as sisters and brothers.

I have a dream today.

I have a dream that one day every valley shall be exalted, every hill and mountain shall be made low, the rough places will be made plain, and the crooked places will be made straight, and the glory of the Lord shall be revealed, and all flesh shall see it together.

This is our hope. This is the faith that I go back to the South with. With this faith we will be able to hew out of the mountain of despair a stone of hope. With this faith we will be able to transform the jangling discords of our nation into a beautiful symphony of brotherhood. With this faith we will be able to work together, to pray together, to struggle together, to go to jail together, to stand up for freedom together, knowing that we will be free one day.

This will be the day when all of God's children will be able to sing with a new meaning, "My country, 'tis of thee, sweet land of liberty, of thee I sing. Land where my fathers died, land of the pilgrim's pride, from every mountainside, let freedom ring."

And if America is to be a great nation this must become true. So let freedom ring from the prodigious hilltops of New Hampshire. Let freedom ring from the mighty mountains of New York. Let freedom ring from the heightening Alleghenies of Pennsylvania!

Let freedom ring from the snowcapped Rockies of Colorado!

Let freedom ring from the curvaceous slopes of California!

But not only that; let freedom ring from Stone Mountain of Georgia!

Let freedom ring from Lookout Mountain of Tennessee!

Let freedom ring from every hill and molehill of Mississippi. From every mountainside, let freedom ring.

And when this happens, when we allow freedom to ring, when we let it ring from every village and every hamlet, from every state and every city, we will be able to speed up that day when all of God's children, black men and white men, Jews and Gentiles, Protestants and Catholics, will be able to join hands and sing in the words of the old Negro spiritual, "Free at last! free at last! thank God Almighty, we are free at last!"

In times of darkness many have taken comfort in the words of the Twenty-third Psalm. Do you have some saying or poem to cling to in times of discouragement?

PSALM 23

David

King James Version

The LORD is my shepherd; I shall not want.

He maketh me to lie down in green pastures: he leadeth me beside the still waters.

He restoreth my soul: he leadeth me in the paths of righteousness for his name's sake.

Yea, though I walk through the valley of the shadow of death,

I will fear no evil: for thou art with me; thy rod and thy staff they comfort me.

Thou preparest a table before me in the presence of mine enemies: thou anointest my head with oil; my cup runneth over.

Surely goodness and mercy shall follow me all the days of my life: and I will dwell in the house of the LORD for ever.

Is your life bigger than this one moment? In the midst of a setback, will you give in to despair or use the wings of your imagination to look ahead to better days?

BE LIKE THE BIRD

Victor Hugo (1802-1885)

Be like the bird that, pausing
in her flight awhile on boughs too slight,
feels them give way beneath her—
yet sings—
knowing she hath wings.

In times of collective despair, will you drag others down or will you train you eyes on the prize and rally those around you?

HENRY V *(Excerpted)*

William Shakespeare (1564–1616)

It is the night of St. Crispen's Day. The year is 1415. The place is a narrow strip of land in the north of France beside the wood of Agincourt.

At dawn, the English troops must engage in battle with a much larger French army. The young King Henry overhears one of his noblemen wishing for more English soldiers. So begins Henry's famous St. Crispen's Day speech in which he urges his men to embrace the opportunity for greatness and to imagine the happy years that will follow their defeat of the much larger French army.

> KING. What's he that wishes so?
> My cousin Westmoreland?
>
> No, my fair cousin;
> If we are marked to die, we are enough
> To do our country loss; and if to live,
> The fewer men, the greater share of honor....
>
> No, faith, my cousin, wish not a man from England.
> God's peace! I would not lose so great an honor
> As one man more methinks would share from me
> For the best hope I have. O, do not wish one more!
>
> Rather proclaim it, Westmoreland, through my host,
> That he which hath no stomach to this fight,
> Let him depart; his passport shall be made,
> And crowns for convoy put into his purse;
> We would not die in that man's company
> That fears his fellowship to die with us.
>
> This day is called the feast of Crispian.
> He that outlives this day, and comes safe home,
> Will stand a tip-toe when this day is named,
> And rouse him at the name of Crispian.

---

* Spelling and obsolete words modernized.

He that shall live this day, and see old age,
Will yearly on the vigil feast his neighbors,
And say "Tomorrow is Saint Crispian."
Then will he strip his sleeve and show his scars,
And say "These wounds I had on Crispian's day."

Old men forget; yet all shall be forgot,
But he'll remember, with advantages,
What feats he did that day. Then shall our names,
Familiar in his mouth as household words—
Harry the King, Bedford and Exeter,
Warwick and Talbot, Salisbury and Gloucester—
Be in their flowing cups freshly remembered.

This story shall the good man teach his son;
And Crispin Crispian shall ne'er go by,
From this day to the ending of the world,
But we in it shall be remembered—
We few, we happy few, we band of brothers;
For he today that sheds his blood with me
Shall be my brother; be he ne'er so vile,
This day shall gentle his condition;
And gentlemen in England now-a-bed
Shall think themselves accursed they were not here,
And hold their manhoods cheap whiles any speaks
That fought with us upon Saint Crispin's day.

The next morning's battle ended in an English victory, known as the Battle of Agincourt.

Ask This

When you feel discouraged, what lifts your spirits? Spending time with friends? Time outdoors? Prayer? Religion? Exercise?

When you are discouraged, do you find yourself turning to temporary fixes that actually cause more trouble in the long run? If so, what are these feel-good fixes that you need to guard against? How can you protect yourself from these false friends?

Try This

This might seem strange, but it helps to prepare for despair: Find a poem, psalm, or short piece of prose that speaks to you and lifts your spirits. Then commit it to memory. Say it every morning for one month. When you write words on your heart in this way, they become part of you and can speak to you when you find yourself in times of trouble.

7

REST

If you have cultivated a heroic spirit, then you aren't afraid of hard work. In fact, you might be so industrious that you neglect one crucial aspect of any long journey: rest.

Without rest, as we press on, day after day, striving and working, we become frazzled. We think less clearly; we make poor decisions; we snap at loved ones. The old saying is true—"All work and no play makes Jack a dull boy." Our senses become dull, our minds and bodies worn down, by constant hard work unleavened by appropriate leisure.

Rest means getting sufficient sleep, but it also means allowing yourself periods of down time, times when you are awake but your brain is allowed to be "off line."

This down time, this time of mental leisure, will pay enormous dividends. Troubles will sink into proper perspective. You will find yourself more in tune with God and your fellow man. Your sense of humor will return. And, when you return to your work, you will find that problems often will be easily resolved now that your mind and creativity have been refreshed. As Leonardo da Vinci said, "Every now and then go away, have a little relaxation, for when you come back to your work your judgment will be surer."

Indeed, creativity researchers have found that creative flashes of insight—the "eureka" moments—often occur during breaks after a long period of concentrated work on a problem (while the person is shaving, for instance, or going for a jog).

With a proper balance of work and leisure, you eventually can learn to carry over certain elements of rest into your work. As theologian Josef Pieper points out, a sense of ongoing rest can allow you to hold things more lightly, to worry less, to be more open and flexible. This contemplative, relaxed attitude helps the hero remain calm even when he enters the storm.

NO REST FOR THE BUILDERS

Jeff Sandefer

Here's a place where I and so many entrepreneurs get stuck on the hero's journey. We hate to rest.

Yes, we understand the genius of taking every seventh day to rest, and we understand the need to reflect and recharge. But days off feel like playing hooky; it's just so hard to escape the pull of the next deal or project. Work brings us energy and being needed makes us feel important and alive. Another seductive trap.

There is such great wisdom in keeping the Sabbath and separating the urgent from the important. And there is such power in praying, meditating, or journaling for thirty minutes each morning. Because it is those small voices that call us to a greatness beyond ourselves. Without them, life becomes busier and busier until the devils of Screwtape win the battle through distraction, weariness, and misdirection.

It's even more important to rest after a great victory. There is nothing more dangerous than a successful entrepreneur who comes to believe that since he or she "made it happen" last time, that he or she can, through force of will, "make it happen" again, without realizing that the "it" is always more a matter of timing, that vision and stubborn determination are powerless without luck and Grace—and applied trial and error.

I wish I could remember who made me promise to keep all of the gains from the sale of my first company in cash for a minimum of twelve months. Not only did that advice save tens of millions of dollars in hubristic bad investments, but it gave me the distance and perspective to realize just how lucky I had been.

That led to the decision to spend a year's sabbatical as a Socratic teacher, to explore with gifted students the decisions that made entrepreneurs and their businesses successful. That was twenty-one years and billions of dollars in investments ago, and I'm still teaching and searching for the answer to the questions of how entrepreneurs and successful companies are made.

So here's a test for you, one I plan to try for myself in the next few months. Can you spend a day alone, in nature, simply resting and reflecting and listening for that small voice that calls you? And if not, what scares you so much about what that voice might say?

DISTRACTION FROM DISTRACTION

Rev. Robert Sirico

I have often wondered if other people have noticed this phenomenon: At the end of sitting in front of a TV set for an evening of scrolling through its various offerings with a remote control, a person comes away from the experience feeling wasted, discontent, and tired, if not also a little guilty for the lost time.

Contract this experience with a person who sits in same chair, in the same location, at the same time and for an equivalent length of time reading a quality book. The same person, I believe, usually comes away from that experience feeling refreshed, enriched; and if somewhat tired, it is that kind of well-earned fatigue that has at its core peace.

What emerges here is the distinction between indolence and rest: the former merely bides time while the latter reflects on meaning and truth; the former depletes while the latter enriches.

Rest is more than the mere conservation of energy. Repose, rest, and leisure remind us that we are all more than the sum total of our material parts.

In the following lines from the Four Quartets, the poet T. S. Elliot could have been referring to our contemporary, multi-tasking culture when he identified the discontent in the human heart that results from distraction:

> "Neither plenitude nor vacancy. Only a flicker
> Over the strained time-ridden faces
> Distracted from distraction by distraction
> Filled with fancies and empty of meaning
> Tumid apathy with no concentration ..."

Think about that third line in particular: "Distracted from distraction by distraction." What a searing insight into the loss of energy that people experience when they fail simply to take time to reflect, contemplate, and replenish their interior resources.

Some people neglect this part of life simply because they are too busy being indolent, channel surfing, "entertaining ourselves death" as Neil Postman put it. But for others of us, the principal way we end up neglecting to replenish ourselves through reflective leisure is that we fill more and more of our time with work. The rationalizations for this behavior are easy enough to come by, of course: "It is for a good cause ... I have to support my family ... Sloth is a vice ... I have lots of opportunities now that I might not have again later."

But these are just that—rationalizations—because they lack balance and, frankly, honesty.

In the ancient world the Jews saw themselves in special covenant with God. Part of that covenant which was not very well understood by the surrounding tribes was the requirement to rest on every seventh day. Some saw this as laziness on their part. But that misses the point of the Sabbath. You see, it is the essence of slavery that there is no rest or relief from it—you are owned lock, stock, and barrel by your taskmaster—whether that taskmaster is a literal slave owner or a figurative one in the form of some job that never stops demanding your attention. But humans were not created for slavery; we were created for stewardship and relationship, purposes that involve creative labor but for which creative labor is not the be all and end all.

It is for this reason that a crucial purpose of Sabbath rest for the people of Israel was not to avoid work but to contemplate it, to look beyond the utility of things to their meaning and purpose, to reflect on what the philosophers might call the *'telos'* or finality of work.

Life, at least human life, cannot be content and satisfying, let alone heroic, if it does not contain a dimension of contemplation and reflection. If *human beings* simply become *human doings*, our sense of ourselves and our existence is diminished, leaving it mediocre, unsatisfying, and meaningless.

How can moments of rest and contemplation soften and enrich your times of work?

DAFFODILS

William Wordsworth (1770-1850)

I wander'd lonely as a cloud
That floats on high o'er vales and hills,
When all at once I saw a crowd,
A host, of golden daffodils;
Beside the lake, beneath the trees,
Fluttering and dancing in the breeze.

Continuous as the stars that shine
And twinkle on the Milky Way,
They stretch'd in never-ending line
Along the margin of a bay:
Ten thousand saw I at a glance,
Tossing their heads in sprightly dance.

The waves beside them danced; but they
Out-did the sparkling waves in glee:
A poet could not but be gay,
In such a jocund company:
I gazed—and gazed—but little thought
What wealth the show to me had brought:

For oft, when on my couch I lie
In vacant or in pensive mood,
They flash upon that inward eye
Which is the bliss of solitude;
And then my heart with pleasure fills,
And dances with the daffodils.

In the biblical account of creation, the Maker of All works hard creating a rich and beautiful world—and then He rests, and commands his creatures to do the same. Does this undermine the modern notion that you or I could be too busy, too important, to take a break?

GENESIS 1:27–2:3
King James Version

So God created man in his own image, in the image of God created he him; male and female created he them.

And God blessed them, and God said unto them, Be fruitful, and multiply, and replenish the earth, and subdue it: and have dominion over the fish of the sea, and over the fowl of the air, and over every living thing that moveth upon the earth.

And God said, Behold, I have given you every herb bearing seed, which is upon the face of all the earth, and every tree, in the which is the fruit of a tree yielding seed; to you it shall be for meat.

And to every beast of the earth, and to every fowl of the air, and to every thing that creepeth upon the earth, wherein there is life, I have given every green herb for meat: and it was so.

And God saw every thing that he had made, and, behold, it was very good. And the evening and the morning were the sixth day.

Thus the heavens and the earth were finished, and all the host of them.

And on the seventh day God ended his work which he had made; and he rested on the seventh day from all his work which he had made.

And God blessed the seventh day, and sanctified it: because that in it he had rested from all his work which God created and made.

Why might it be useful for the hero to be still and contemplate a higher power?

PSALM 46 *(Excerpted)*
King James Version

God is our refuge and strength, a very present help in trouble.

Therefore will not we fear, though the earth be removed, and though the mountains be carried into the midst of the sea; Though the waters thereof roar and be troubled, though the mountains shake with the swelling thereof.

There is a river, the streams whereof shall make glad the city of God, the holy place of the tabernacles of the most High. God is in the midst of her; she shall not be moved: God shall help her, and that right early....

He maketh wars to cease unto the end of the earth; he breaketh the bow, and cutteth the spear in sunder; he burneth the chariot in the fire.

Be still, and know that I am God.

Even if we are doing work we enjoy, can too much busy-ness dissipate our powers?

COME, REST AWHILE

Lucy Maud Montgomery (1874–1942)

Come, rest awhile, and let us idly stray
In glimmering valleys, cool and far away.

Come from the greedy mart, the troubled street,
And listen to the music, faint and sweet.

That echoes ever to a listening ear,
Unheard by those who will not pause to hear

The wayward chimes of memory's pensive bells,
Wind-blown o'er misty hills and curtained dells.

One step aside and dewy buds unclose
The sweetness of the violet and the rose;

Song and romance still linger in the green,
Emblossomed ways by you so seldom seen,

And near at hand, would you but see them, lie
All lovely things beloved in days gone by.

You have forgotten what it is to smile
In your too busy life. Come, rest awhile.

Pilgrim's Progress *is perhaps the most famous tale about a hero's journey. Throughout this story the main character and his fellow pilgrims face many trials and dangers; however, they also frequently take time to rest. Sometimes they rest and sleep, sometimes they rest and eat, and sometimes—as in this selection—they use a time of rest to pray.*

Are different sorts of rest necessary at different moments in your hero's journey? How can you ensure that you always use your rest time well?

THE PILGRIM'S PROGRESS

John Bunyan (1628–1688)

Retold by Mary Macgregor

Christiana sets out on a journey to the Holy City, following in the footsteps of her husband Christian. She takes their four sons with her. Along the way they meet Mr. Greatheart, who agrees to go with them as guide and protector.

Now they drew towards the end of the valley, and just there, out of a cave, came forth Maul, a giant. This giant used to flatter and spoil young pilgrims.

When the giant saw Mr. Greatheart, he said to him, "How often have you been forbidden to do these things?"

"What things?" said Mr. Greatheart.

"What things!" answered the giant, "you know what things, but I will put an end to your doings," and he prepared to fight.

"But," said Mr. Greatheart, "before we begin, let us know why we must fight."

Now the women and children stood trembling and knew not what to do.

Then said the giant, "Thou art a kidnapper, for thou gatherest together women and children, and carriest them into a strange country, and so thou makest my master's kingdom weaker."

"I am commanded to do all I can to bring men, women, and children out of thy master's kingdom, for thy master is Satan," said Mr. Greatheart.

Then the giant came up, and Mr. Greatheart went to meet him, and as he went he drew his sword, but the giant had a club.

At the first blow, Maul, the giant, struck Mr. Greatheart down upon one of his knees. When the women and children saw that, they cried.

So their guide got up again and gave the giant a wound in his arm. Thus they fought for about an hour, then they sat down to rest, but Mr. Greatheart began to pray. Also the women and children did nothing but sigh and cry all the time the battle did last.

When they had rested and taken breath they both began again, and Mr. Greatheart with a blow brought the giant down to the ground. Then he ran to him and pierced him under the ribs, till the giant began to faint and could hold up his club no longer. So Mr. Greatheart smote the head of the giant from his shoulders.

Then the women and children rejoiced, and Greatheart also rejoiced, and praised God for His help.

Ask This

Do you make time for sufficient rest and leisure in your life?

Do electronic devices (cell phones, e-mail, text messages) prevent you from being able to step away for awhile, to rest and recuperate?

A wise man once said, "No one is indispensible." Can you be humble enough to admit that the work world can function without you every now and then, to allow yourself time to rest?

Try This

This weekend or the next, choose one day to turn off all your electronic communication equipment. Silence the ringers on your phones. Leave the computer and cell phones off. Let yourself enter deep into the silence knowing that you will not be jerked back into the weekday stresses. Let the important—your physical, mental, emotional, and spiritual wellbeing, and those of your loved ones—take precedence over the urgent.

8

FIGHTING THE DRAGON

If you are pursuing a hero's quest, the time will come when you must face a life-changing challenge. This is not a stone in the road; this is a man-eating, fire-breathing dragon. You will not escape unscathed. You will not emerge unchanged. You must sacrifice part of yourself in order to conquer and move forward.

When this great fight comes, you will succeed only if you have prepared in advance for the moment. Assess your battle readiness by asking these questions:

Have you developed your strength by facing and overcoming various obstacles along the road?

Have you developed wisdom by practicing self-discipline and heeding your ethical guardrails?

Have you learned to persevere, to try one method after another until you find success?

Have you learned to use your imagination in order to keep your eyes fixed on the prize, even and especially when you are facing danger?

If you can answer yes to these questions, then you are prepared to fight whatever dragon may come. You have a good chance of reaching your goal.

And what if you don't? Do heroes ever lose, falling beneath the enemy's sword, the monster's teeth? Of course they do; and so might you.

But if you are well prepared, you won't lose in the ways that matter most. You won't dishonor yourself, your dream, your companions, or your God. You will be faithful to the end, and in doing so, even in defeat you will triumph.

BEFORE THE DRAGON ARRIVES

Rev. Robert Sirico

Diet (pronounced "Deet") Eman was only twenty years old when she began resisting Hitler's "Final Solution" against the Jews in Nazi-occupied Holland during World War II. She and her fiancé, Hein Sietsma, started smuggling Jews into the surrounding countryside, hiding them with farmers—sixty Jews in the first two weeks alone, eventually hundreds.

Then Diet and Hein also began arranging false identification cards in order to more safely transport the Jews to their hiding places out in the country. By 1943 the group that Diet worked with needed eight hundred cards a month.

The whole enterprise was dangerous. It easily could have cost Diet Eman her life. It did cost the life of her fiancé, Hein Sietsma. He was intercepted by the Nazis and deported to the Dachau concentration camp, where he died. And yet, even as Diet grieved, she went right on helping the Jews.

Where did she find the courage? What inspired her to give up so much and to risk so much for people she did not know, whose religious faith she did not share, whose ethnicity was different from her own? What could inspire a person to do a thing like that?

I was able to ask the question directly to Diet Eman, now ninety-one years old, because she survived the war and immigrated to America and to the same corner of the Great Lakes region where I live and work. We were together at a public gathering and I took the opportunity to ask her why she had risked so much, and had she been afraid.

Diet said, "Yes, you were in fear. You never knew in the morning whether you would be free in the evening." She went on to say, "I always feel funny when people applaud me for what I did because if you love God and love Jesus, you would have done the same, so it's nothing special."

Her words led me to an insight about the nature of the heroic. Diet's secret was that she had decided, long before the crisis came, what was right and what was wrong. She had not waited for a dragon to arrive before she set about practicing moral courage.

To paraphrase one ancient Jewish writer, from her youth she had carved what was right onto the tablets of her heart. That is why she could speak of what she felt she "had to do" as though it were not a big thing. By the time the crisis arrived, her convictions, her habits of moral courage, were so deeply rooted in her that she didn't think twice about doing what was necessary to fight a great evil and protect those who were being hunted and killed.

After Diet had answered my question, she looked at me and asked her own question. "What if this had happened to you?" she said. And then, in her simple manner, added, "So we must do unto others. And you may be scared stiff, but you do what God asks."

WHEN WILL YOUR DRAGON APPEAR?

Jeff Sandefer

Here's the good news—and trust me, it is good news, however it may sound: You have your own special dragon you are meant to slay in order to advance on your journey, and you have the talents and courage needed to slay it.

Here's the bad news: If you refuse to face this dragon, it will keep turning up in the oddest of places, at the worst of times.

Your dragon will be the biggest challenge you must face, at least at this stage of your journey. No mere stone in the road, the dragon requires you to sacrifice a part of yourself to defeat it, in ways that will feel like death itself. That's what makes slaying the dragon so difficult and so powerful.

Sound like some sort of psycho-drama? It won't when you face a dragon for real.

My first dragon was about money and power. I had been raised all my life to worship those things above all else, in a way that weakened my soul and cheapened even the most legitimate accomplishment.

Fighting this dragon was all-consuming. I was only able to lay it in the dust after the financial windfall from my first business. The windfall itself didn't do it—it was just fuel for the dragon. But I had promised someone that I wouldn't invest the profits for a year, which meant that for a full year I had world enough and time to face that dragon. I held still, looked it in the eye, and in that long moment it became obvious to even a fool like me that money was not the road to happiness, satisfaction, or fulfillment (and if you feel otherwise, trust me, you will find yourself as disappointed as I did when you become rich).

Then came the dragon of "being right." It took many years of hard practice as a Socratic teacher to put this dragon down. And every now and then, along with the money and power dragon, he revives and tries to rear his ugly head. But time and practice and habit make it easier and easier to put both in their proper places.

What's my next dragon? I'm not sure. Possibly the fear of death and decline, though there may be other dragons before I face that one.

Searching for that next dragon, that next great encounter that is much more than a simple stone in the road ahead, is both frightening and exhilarating, not because it might kill me but because each time, I don't know if I will have the courage to face it.

So each dragon is a test of what I am made of; and the knowledge that another dragon lies in wait somewhere down the road motivates me to keep striving for another helping of strength and wisdom.

If you choose to be brave and noble regardless of what dangers and troubles you face, are you in some important respect a conqueror?

INVICTUS

William Ernest Henley (1849–1903)

Out of the night that covers me,
    Black as the Pit from pole to pole,
I thank whatever gods may be
    For my unconquerable soul.

In the fell clutch of circumstance
    I have not winced nor cried aloud,
Under the bludgeonings of chance
    My head is bloody, but unbowed.

Beyond this place of wrath and tears
    Looms but the horror of the shade,
And yet the menace of the years
    Finds, and shall find me, unafraid.

It matters not how strait the gate,
    How charged with punishments the scroll,
I am the master of my fate:
    I am the captain of my soul.

When Nelson Mandela attempted to end South Africa's apartheid system of racially based division and discrimination, he was imprisoned for twenty-seven years. While in prison he continued to work for equality, and his reputation around the world grew.

Four years after his release he was elected President of South Africa and served for five years (1994–1999). He also was awarded the Nobel Peace Prize in 1993.

In 2007 Mandela was interviewed by *Reader's Digest*. The magazine noted that throughout his many years in prison, Mandela "refused to let his spirit be broken."

The interviewer asked, "When you were in prison all those long years on Robben Island and elsewhere, was there something that came back to you, something you had either in your mind, a message or passage from a book, a song, something that helped sustain you and keep up your spirits?"

Mandela replied, "There was a poem by an English poet, W. E. Henley, called 'Invictus.' The last lines go: 'It matters not how straight the gate, How charged with punishments the scroll, I am the master of my fate: I am the captain of my soul.'" Reading such words "puts life in you," Mandela says.

In 2009 a biographical movie of Nelson Mandela's life was released; its title is *Invictus*.

Are you brave enough to fight a mighty battle alone, if need be? Are you willing to come to someone else's aid, even if no one else does?

BEOWULF

Old English Poem (circa 700-1000)

Retold by Hamilton Wright Mabie

In due time Beowulf himself became King, and well he governed the land for fifty years. Then trouble came.

A slave, fleeing from his master, stumbled by an evil chance into the den of a dragon. There he saw a dazzling hoard of gold, guarded by the dragon for three hundred winters. The treasure tempted him, and he carried off a tankard of gold to give to his master, to make peace with him.

The dragon had been sleeping, now he awoke, and sniffed the scent of an enemy along the rock.

Presently the sun sank, and the dragon had his will. He set forth, burning all the cheerful homes of men: his rage was felt far and wide. Before dawn he shot back again to his dark home, trusting in his mound and in his craft to defend himself.

Now Beowulf heard that his own home had been burnt to the ground. His breast heaved with anger. He meant to rid his country of the plague, and to fight the dragon single handed. He would have thought it shame to seek him with a large band, he who, as a lad, had killed Grendel and his kin. As he armed for the fray, many thoughts filled his mind; he remembered the days of his youth and manhood. "I fought many wars in my youth," he said, "and now that I am aged, and the keeper of my people, I will yet again seek the enemy and do famously."

He bade his men await him on the mountain-side. They were to see which of the two would come alive out of the tussle.

There the aged King beheld where a rocky archway stood, with a stream of fire gushing from it; no one could stand there and not be scorched. He gave a great shout, and the dragon answered with a hot breath of flame.

Beowulf, with drawn sword, stood well up to his shield, when the burning dragon, curved like an arch, came headlong upon him. The shield saved him but little; he swung up the sword to smite the horrible monster, but its edge did not bite. Sparks flew around him on every side; he saw that the end of his days had come.

His men crept away to the woods to save their lives. One, and one only, Wiglaf by name, sped through the smoke and flame to help his lord.

"My Lord Beowulf!" he cried, "with all your might defend life, I will support you to the utmost."

The dragon came on in fury; in a trice the flames consumed Wiglaf's shield, but, nothing daunted, he stepped under the shelter of Beowulf's as his own fell in ashes about him. The King remembered his strength of old, and he smote with his sword with such force that it stuck in the monster's head, while splinters flew all around. His hand was so strong that, as men used to say, he broke any sword in using it, and was none the worse for it.

Now, for the third time, the dragon rushed upon him, and seized him by the neck with his poisonous fangs. Wiglaf, with no thought for himself, rushed forward, though he was scorched with the flames, and smote the dragon lower down than Beowulf had done. With such effect the sword entered the dragon's body that from that moment the fire began to cease.

The King, recovering his senses, drew his knife and ended the monster's life. So these two together destroyed the enemy of the people. To Beowulf that was the greatest moment of his life, when he saw his work completed.

The wound that the dragon had given him began to burn and swell, for the poison had entered it. He knew that the tale of his days was told. As he rested on a stone by the mound, he pondered thoughtfully, looking on the cunning work of the dwarfs of old, the stone arches on their rocky pillars. Wiglaf, with tender care, unloosed his helmet and brought him water.

The brave King took from his neck his golden collar, took his helmet and his coronet, and gave them to his true knight, Wiglaf. "Fate has swept all my kinsmen away," said he, "and now I must follow them."

That was his last word, as his soul departed from his bosom, to join the company of the just. Of all Kings in the world, he was, said his men, the gentlest to his knights and the most desirous of honour.

What is worth fighting for?

GIVE ME LIBERTY OR GIVE ME DEATH

Patrick Henry (1736-1799)

On March 23, 1775 the Virginia Convention debated whether to pass a resolution arming Virginia's militia in support of the colonies' struggle for independence from Britain. On that day Patrick Henry made a rousing speech that swung the decision in favor of arming the troops. His speech was not written down, but various men later wrote what they recalled. Here is a portion:

They tell us, sir, that we are weak; unable to cope with so formidable an adversary. But when shall we be stronger? Will it be the next week, or the next year? Will it be when we are totally disarmed, and when a British guard shall be stationed in every house?

Shall we gather strength by irresolution and inaction? Shall we acquire the means of effectual resistance by lying supinely on our backs and hugging the delusive phantom of hope, until our enemies shall have bound us hand and foot?

Sir, we are not weak if we make a proper use of those means which the God of nature hath placed in our power. The millions of people, armed in the holy cause of liberty, and in such a country as that which we possess, are invincible by any force which our enemy can send against us.

Besides, sir, we shall not fight our battles alone. There is a just God who presides over the destinies of nations, and who will raise up friends to fight our battles for us. The battle, sir, is not to the strong alone; it is to the vigilant, the active, the brave.

Besides, sir, we have no election. If we were base enough to desire it, it is now too late to retire from the contest. There is no retreat but in submission and slavery! Our chains are forged! Their clanking may be heard on the plains of Boston! The war is inevitable—and let it come! I repeat it, sir, let it come.

It is in vain, sir, to extenuate the matter. Gentlemen may cry, Peace, Peace—but there is no peace. The war is actually begun! The next gale that sweeps from the north will bring to our ears the clash of resounding arms! Our brethren are already in the field! Why stand we here idle? What is it that gentlemen wish? What would they have?

Is life so dear, or peace so sweet, as to be purchased at the price of chains and slavery? Forbid it, Almighty God! I know not what course others may take; but as for me, give me liberty or give me death!

In this tale, a young man is prepared for battle in his own way and refuses to be diverted into using other people's methods. Are you confident and comfortable with your own preparations?

DAVID AND GOLIATH *(Excerpted)*

1 Samuel 17

King James Version

Now the Philistines gathered together their armies to battle. And the Philistines stood on a mountain on the one side, and Saul and the men of Israel stood on a mountain on the other side: and there was a valley between them.

And there went out a champion out of the camp of the Philistines, named Goliath, of Gath, whose height was six cubits and a span. And he had an helmet of brass upon his head, and he was armed with a coat of mail; and the weight of the coat was five thousand shekels of brass. And he had greaves of brass upon his legs, and a target of brass between his shoulders. And the staff of his spear was like a weaver's beam; and his spear's head weighed six hundred shekels of iron: and one bearing a shield went before him.

And he stood and cried unto the armies of Israel, and said unto them, Why are ye come out to set your battle in array? Am not I a Philistine, and ye servants to Saul? Choose you a man for you, and let him come down to me. If he be able to fight with me, and to kill me, then will we be your servants: but if I prevail against him, and kill him, then shall ye be our servants, and serve us. And the Philistine said, I defy the armies of Israel this day; give me a man, that we may fight together.

When Saul and all Israel heard those words of the Philistine, they were dismayed, and greatly afraid.

And the three eldest sons of Jesse went and followed Saul to the battle. And David was the youngest. But David went and returned from Saul to feed his father's sheep at Bethlehem.

And the Philistine drew near morning and evening, and presented himself forty days.

And Jesse said unto David his son, Take now for thy brethren an ephah of this parched corn, and these ten loaves, and run to the camp of thy brethren; and carry these ten cheeses unto the captain of their thousand, and look how thy brethren fare, and take their pledge.

And David rose up early in the morning, and left the sheep with a keeper, and went, as Jesse had commanded him, and ran into the army, and came and saluted his brethren. And as he talked with them, behold, there came up the champion, the Philistine of Gath, Goliath by name, out of the armies of the Philistines, and spake according to the same words: and David heard them.

And all the men of Israel, when they saw the man, fled from him, and were sore afraid. And the men of Israel said, Have ye seen this man that is come up? Surely to defy Israel is he come up: and it shall be, that the man who killeth him, the king will enrich him with great riches, and will give him his daughter, and make his father's house free in Israel.

And David's words were rehearsed before Saul: and he sent for him.

And David said to Saul, Let no man's heart fail because of him; thy servant will go and fight with this Philistine.

And Saul said to David, Thou art not able to go against this Philistine to fight with him: for thou art but a youth, and he a man of war from his youth.

And David said unto Saul, Thy servant kept his father's sheep, and there came a lion, and a bear, and took a lamb out of the flock: And I went out after him, and smote him, and delivered it out of his mouth: and when he arose against me, I caught him by his beard, and smote him, and slew him. Thy servant slew both the lion and the bear: and this uncircumcised Philistine shall be as one of them, seeing he hath defied the armies of the living God.

David said moreover, The LORD that delivered me out of the paw of the lion, and out of the paw of the bear, he will deliver me out of the hand of this Philistine. And Saul said unto David, Go, and the LORD be with thee.

And Saul armed David with his armour, and he put an helmet of brass upon his head; also he armed him with a coat of mail. And David girded his sword upon his armour, and he assayed to go; for he had not proved it. And David said unto Saul, I cannot go with these; for I have not proved them. And David put them off him.

And he took his staff in his hand, and chose him five smooth stones out of the brook, and put them in a shepherd's bag which he had, even in a scrip; and his sling was in his hand: and he drew near to the Philistine.

And the Philistine came on and drew near unto David; and the man that bare the shield went before him. And when the Philistine looked about, and saw David, he disdained him: for he was but a youth, and ruddy, and of a fair countenance. And the Philistine said unto David, Am I a dog, that thou comest to me with staves? And the Philistine cursed David by his gods.

And the Philistine said to David, Come to me, and I will give thy flesh unto the fowls of the air, and to the beasts of the field.

Then said David to the Philistine, Thou comest to me with a sword, and with a spear, and with a shield: but I come to thee in the name of the LORD of hosts, the God of the armies of Israel, whom thou hast defied.

This day will the LORD deliver thee into mine hand; and I will smite thee, and take thine head from thee; and I will give the carcasses of the host of the Philistines this day unto the fowls of the air, and to the wild beasts of the earth; that all the earth may know that there is a God in Israel. And all this assembly shall know that the LORD saveth not with sword and spear: for the battle is the LORD's, and he will give you into our hands.

And it came to pass, when the Philistine arose, and came, and drew nigh to meet David, that David hastened, and ran toward the army to meet the Philistine. And David put his hand in his bag, and took thence a stone, and slang it, and smote the Philistine in his forehead, that the stone sunk into his forehead; and he fell upon his face to the earth.

So David prevailed over the Philistine with a sling and with a stone, and smote the Philistine, and slew him; but there was no sword in the hand of David.

Therefore David ran, and stood upon the Philistine, and took his sword, and drew it out of the sheath thereof, and slew him, and cut off his head therewith. And when the Philistines saw their champion was dead, they fled.

Do you agree with Thomas Paine—that what we attain too cheaply, we esteem lightly? Have you fought hard to attain something that you still esteem highly?

The American Crisis, Essay 1 *(Excerpted)*

Thomas Paine (1737-1809)

During the time of the Revolutionary War, Thomas Paine wrote a series of essays in support of an independent and self-governing United States. General Washington ordered the following essay to be read to the Continental troops on December 23, 1776—two days before the famous Christmas Day crossing of the Delaware.

These are the times that try men's souls. The summer soldier and the sunshine patriot will, in this crisis, shrink from the service of their country; but he that stands by it now, deserves the love and thanks of man and woman.

Tyranny, like hell, is not easily conquered; yet we have this consolation with us, that the harder the conflict, the more glorious the triumph. What we obtain too cheap, we esteem too lightly: it is dearness only that gives every thing its value. Heaven knows how to put a proper price upon its goods; and it would be strange indeed if so celestial an article as FREEDOM should not be highly rated.

Britain, with an army to enforce her tyranny, has declared that she has a right (not only to TAX) but "to BIND us in ALL CASES WHATSOEVER" and if being bound in that manner, is not slavery, then is there not such a thing as slavery upon earth. Even the expression is impious; for so unlimited a power can belong only to God....

I have as little superstition in me as any man living, but my secret opinion has ever been, and still is, that God Almighty will not give up a people to military destruction, or leave them unsupportedly to perish, who have so earnestly and so repeatedly sought to avoid the calamities of war, by every decent method which wisdom could invent....

I shall not now attempt to give all the particulars of our retreat to the Delaware; suffice it for the present to say, that both officers and men, though greatly harassed and fatigued, frequently without rest, covering, or provision, the inevitable consequences of a long retreat, bore it with a manly and martial spirit. All their wishes centered in one, which was, that the country would turn out and help them to drive the enemy back.

Voltaire has remarked that King William never appeared to full advantage but in difficulties and in action; the same remark may be made on General Washington, for the character fits him. There is a natural firmness in some minds which cannot be unlocked by trifles, but which, when unlocked, discovers a cabinet of fortitude; and I reckon it among those kind of public blessings, which we do not immediately see, that God hath blessed him with uninterrupted health, and given him a mind that can even flourish upon care.

... I once felt all that kind of anger, which a man ought to feel, against the mean principles that are held by the Tories: a noted one, who kept a tavern at Amboy, was standing at his door, with as pretty a child in his hand, about eight or nine years old, as I ever saw, and after speaking his mind as freely as he thought was prudent, finished with this unfatherly expression, "Well! give me peace in my day."

Not a man lives on the continent but fully believes that a separation must some time or other finally take place, and a generous parent should have said, "If there must be trouble, let it be in my day, that my child may have peace;" and this single reflection, well applied, is sufficient to awaken every man to duty.

Not a place upon earth might be so happy as America. Her situation is remote from all the wrangling world, and she has nothing to do but to trade with them. A man can distinguish himself between temper and principle, and I am as confident, as I am that God governs the world, that America will never be happy till she gets clear of foreign dominion. Wars, without ceasing, will break out till that period arrives, and the continent must in the end be conqueror; for though the flame of liberty may sometimes cease to shine, the coal can never expire.

America did not, nor does not want force; but she wanted a proper application of that force. Wisdom is not the purchase of a day, and it is no wonder that we should err at the first setting off. From an excess of tenderness, we were unwilling to raise an army, and trusted our cause to the temporary defense of a well-meaning militia.

A summer's experience has now taught us better; yet with those troops, while they were collected, we were able to set bounds to the progress of the enemy, and, thank God! they are again assembling.... Say not that thousands are gone, turn out your tens of thousands; throw not the burden of the day upon Providence, but "show your faith by your works," that God may bless you.

It matters not where you live, or what rank of life you hold, the evil or the blessing will reach you all. The far and the near, the home counties and the back, the rich and the poor, will suffer or rejoice alike.

The heart that feels not now is dead; the blood of his children will curse his cowardice, who shrinks back at a time when a little might have saved the whole, and made them happy.

I love the man that can smile in trouble, that can gather strength from distress, and grow brave by reflection. 'Tis the business of little minds to shrink; but he whose heart is firm, and whose conscience approves his conduct, will pursue his principles unto death.

Ask This

Perhaps you'll never be called to risk your life for someone or something. But if it came to that, do you think there is anything worth risking your life for? What?

Now take it down a step. What are some things you wouldn't die for, but would be willing to fight hard for?

In what ways can you fight for these people, ideals, or achievements?

Try This

Certain groups of people—police officers, soldiers, rescue workers—routinely risk their lives for others or for a noble cause. Talk to someone belonging to one of these groups. Ask what he or she believes is worth fighting for, even dying for.

9

COMING HOME

The road has been long and weary; the stones have bruised your feet; but the dragons have been conquered—at least for now—and you finally have arrived at your destination. You're home.

What now?

Now you can take time to enjoy the success you have earned. Look around; see what you've done. See what others have helped you do. See how you've been blessed. Take time, in short, to be thankful. Take time to be grateful.

Also take time to use your success not just for yourself, but for others. This applies whether we're talking about money and influence, or patience, wisdom, and love. Enrich the soil of your homeland by every means available. Invest in the future.

And while you are home, take the time to ask yourself some hard questions. Do you have regrets? Have you compromised in ways you should not have? In what ways did you make yourself proud? Is your success the sort that endures?

Finally, while you are home, consider where you would like to go next, for unless you have reached the end of life's journey, you will soon set out on another adventure.

Why? Because, like Tennyson's Ulysses, you are the sort who says, "How dull it is to pause, to make an end, to rust unburnished, not to shine in use!"

You are a striver, an achiever. You are determined to make the most of every minute of your life, of every talent you've been given, of every skill you have achieved.

You will soon set forth again.

Don't set out without a plan. Return once more—and again and again, at the end of each journey—to that fundamental question: Who are you, and who would you like to become?

THE END GAME

Jeff Sandefer

So what is the end goal? Why am I here?

In my twenties, the end goal was all about worldly success. Sure, I thought about politics or saving the world, but they were far-off goals, reserved for after I had earned plenty of money. Later I came to realize that my longing for material success was more about becoming the master of my own destiny. Both goals would prove to be poor masters.

Don't get me wrong, having money, while it comes with its own set of problems, is far better than being poor. And there's nothing more freeing than making more money than you spend, so that your time belongs to you. But in chasing the dream of being able to wholly control my destiny, I was chasing a mirage. Such control is impossible.

I admire those with enough inborn wisdom to be comfortable with this fact. I had to climb the peaks of money and power to learn this lesson and find more meaningful challenges to overcome.

The fact that I learned this in and through my entrepreneurial ventures is part of why I have little patience with pundits who trivialize the aspirations of the entrepreneur. We each have our own road to travel, stones to plow through, and dragons to fight, and that's as it should be.

What I have found is that the end of each hero's journey gives you the right to play on another level—stronger, more tested, with more finely honed talents, instincts, and a more powerful and trusted network of fellow travelers. In other words, each successful journey gives you the chance to make an even bigger impact.

But in the end, it's not about that.

It's about becoming who you were meant to be, in service to the others, and for me, ultimately submitting to my God and Savior. This process of personal growth that comes through the blood, sweat, and courage of journeying heroically, a process at the heart of all the great quest stories, is in the end what gives the hero's journey its power, permanence, and beauty.

SUCCESS

Rev. Robert Sirico

So now you're home. You're finished with one enterprise, and you haven't yet begun on the next. Look around you. What have you achieved?

It might surprise some people to learn that even the Bible—with its ragged prophets living in the wilderness, its wayfaring pilgrims in the desert, its martyrs and saints—doesn't condemn professional success or wealth creation. In fact, the Parable of the Talents (which you read in chapter 2) praises those who used money to make more money.

The danger with money and success—according to both the Bible and many other religious and philosophical teachings—is that they can become all-consuming.

They can keep us from loving our families as we ought; can tempt us to violate our ethics and damage our integrity; can hinder us from living a full spiritual life. If we come to love success and material wealth more than we love anything else—family, God, integrity—then wealth has become our master rather than our servant, an idol that we bow down to. It has conquered us.

To keep any potential fame or fortune from becoming our master, we must reflect on other forms of success. What would it mean to be a successful mentor and inspiration to those you lead? What would it mean to be a successful employee? A successful parent? A successful spouse? A successful philanthropist?

Many of these definitions will involve descriptions not of what you gain, but of what you become. Have you become someone who is trustworthy in every situation? Have you become someone who can stay calm in a crisis? Have you become someone who can endure? Have you used your God-given talents to the best of your ability?

These character virtues will help you cope with material success in a positive way; but more than that, they are, ultimately, far more important than any material success. As we all know, "You can't take it with you" when it comes to money, cars, houses, or land. And yet those of us who are convinced that life does not end with the grave also believe that there is something you can take home with you: everything good you have become.

Christians sometimes say it like this: "One short life; it will soon be past. Only things done for Christ will last."

Your final, eternal homecoming must not be ignored, as you make your calculations and your plans. Live in such a way—journey in such a way—that, when your life on this earth is ended, you will be greeted in the heavenly realms with those blessed words, "Well done, thou good and faithful servant."

As you rest and look back on your endeavors, consider what forms of success, besides material wealth, you have achieved.

HIGH FLIGHT

John Gillespie Magee, Jr. (1922-1941)

Oh! I have slipped the surly bonds of Earth
And danced the skies on laughter-silvered wings;
Sunward I've climbed, and joined the tumbling mirth
of sun-split clouds,—and done a hundred things
You have not dreamed of—wheeled and soared and swung
High in the sunlit silence. Hov'ring there,
I've chased the shouting wind along, and flung
My eager craft through footless halls of air ...
Up, up the long, delirious, burning blue
I've topped the wind-swept heights with easy grace
Where never lark nor even eagle flew—
And, while with silent lifting mind I've trod
The high untrespassed sanctity of space,
Put out my hand, and touched the face of God.

Note: John Gillespie Magee was a pilot who wrote this poem shortly before he died (age 19) in a mid-air collision. The first and last lines of his poem are engraved on his tombstone.

The deepest measure of your success will be this: in what ways did you bless the world you left behind?

AND YET FOOLS SAY

George Sanford Holmes (1883-1955)

He captured light and caged it in a glass,
Then harnessed it forever to a wire;

He gave men robots with no backs to tire
In bearing burdens for the toiling mass.

He freed the tongue in wood and wax and brass,
Imbued dull images with motion's fire,

Transmuted metal into human choir
These man-made miracles he brought to pass.

Bulbs banish night along the Great White Way,
Thin threads of copper throb with might unseen;

On silver curtains shadow-actors play
That walk and talk from magic-mouthed machine,

While continents converse through skies o'erhead
And yet fools say that Edison is dead!

What sort of person can work hard, not merely to enjoy the fruits of his labor, but to plant fruit for other people to enjoy? Are you that sort of person?

THE BRIDGE BUILDER

Will Allen Dromgoole (1860-1931)

An old man, going a lone highway,
Came, at the evening, cold and gray,
To a chasm, vast, and deep, and wide,
Through which was flowing a sullen tide.
The old man crossed in the twilight dim;
The sullen stream had no fears for him;
But he turned, when safe on the other side,
And built a bridge to span the tide.

"Old man," said a fellow pilgrim, near,
"You are wasting strength with building here;
Your journey will end with the ending day;
You never again must pass this way;
You have crossed the chasm, deep and wide,
Why build you the bridge at the eventide?"

The builder lifted his old gray head:
"Good friend, in the path I have come," he said,
"There followeth after me today
A youth, whose feet must pass this way.
This chasm, that has been naught to me,
To that fair-haired youth may a pitfall be.
He, too, must cross in the twilight dim;
Good friend, I am building the bridge for him."

Whether we journey or rest at home, we can be calm and confident if we know who we are and whom we serve.

CROSSING THE BAR

Alfred, Lord Tennyson (1809-1892)

Sunset and evening star,
And one clear call for me!
And may there be no moaning of the bar,
When I put out to sea,

But such a tide as moving seems asleep,
Too full for sound and foam,
When that which drew from out the boundless deep
Turns again home.

Twilight and evening bell,
And after that the dark!
And may there be no sadness of farewell,
When I embark;

For tho' from out our bourne of Time and Place
The flood may bear me far,
I hope to see my Pilot face to face
When I have crossed the bar.

A FAREWELL

Charles Kingsley (1819-1875)

My fairest child, I have no song to give you;
No lark could pipe to skies so dull and gray;
Yet, ere we part, one lesson I can leave you
For every day.

Be good, sweet maid, and let who will be clever;
Do noble things, not dream them all day long:
And so make life, death, and that vast forever
One grand, sweet song.

Ask This

What would you like to see written on your tombstone? That isn't a morbid question, but one intended to help you focus on the things in life that have enduring value.

What character attributes would you like to have by the time you reach your goals?

What positive character attributes might success itself enhance?

What positive character attributes might success undermine if you aren't vigilant?

Try This

Imagine that yesterday your every dream came true, every ambition was fulfilled. If this were the case, how would your life be different than it is now? How would *you* be different?

And what would you choose to do today?

WORKS CITED

Note: Many of these works are available online.

Aesop. "The Crow and the Pitcher." *For the Children's Hour*. Edited by Carolyn S. Bailey and Clara M. Lewis. Springfield, Massachusetts: Milton Bradley Company, 1915.

———. "The Farmer and His Sons." *Fairy Stories and Fables*. Edited by James Baldwin. New York: American Book Company, 1895.

———. "The Farmer's Sons." *The Aesop for Children*. Chicago: Rand McNally, 1919.

———. "The Fox and the Goat." *The Aesop for Children*, Chicago: Rand McNally, 1919.

———. "The Lark and Her Young Ones." *The Aesop for Children*. Chicago: Rand McNally, 1919.

———. "The Travelers and the Bear." *The Book of Fables and Folk Stories*. Edited by Horace E. Scudder. Boston: Houghton Mifflin Company, 1915.

Arnold, Sarah. "The Stone in the Road." *For the Children's Hour*. Edited by Carolyn S. Bailey and Clara M. Lewis. Springfield, Massachusetts: Milton Bradley Company, 1915.

Bailey, Carolyn S. "Apple-Seed John." *For the Children's Hour*. Edited by Carolyn S. Bailey and Clara M. Lewis. Springfield, Massachusetts: Milton Bradley Company, 1915.

Baum, L. Frank. *The Wonderful Wizard of Oz.*

"Beowulf." *Legends Every Child Should Know*. Edited by Hamilton Wright Mabie. New York: Gosset & Dunlap, 1906.

Buechner, Frederick. "Vocation." *Wishful Thinking: A Seeker's ABC*. HarperOne, 1993.

Bunyan, John. *The Pilgrim's Progress*. Modernized by Mary Macgregor. *Stories from the Pilgrim's Progress*. New York: E.P. Dutton & Co., 1907.

Churchill, Winston. "Blood, Toil, Tears, and Sweat." England. May 13, 1940. Speech.

———. "Never Give In." Harrow School. England. October 29, 1941. Speech.

———. "We Shall Fight." House of Commons. England. June 4, 1940. Speech.

"Do What You Can." *For the Children's Hour*. Edited by Carolyn S. Bailey and Clara M. Lewis. Springfield, Massachusetts: Milton Bradley Company, 1915.

Dromgoole, Will Allen. "The Bridge Builder."

Guest, Edgar A. "Can't."

———. "Things Not Done Before."

Hawthorne, Nathaniel. "The Golden Touch." *A Wonder-Book for Girls and Boys*, 1852.

Henley, William Ernest. "Invictus."

Henry, Patrick. "Give Me Liberty or Give Me Death."

Holmes, George S. "And Yet Fools Say."

Hugo, Victor. "Be Like the Bird."

King, Martin Luther, Jr. "I Have a Dream." Lincoln Memorial, Washington, D.C. August 28, 1963. Speech.

Kingsley, Charles. "A Farewell."

Longfellow, Henry Wadsworth. "A Psalm of Life."

Magee, John Gillespie. "High Flight."

Mandela, Nelson. Interview by *Readers Digest*. "Face to Face." October 2007.

Montgomery, Lucy Maud. "Come, Rest Awhile."

Niemöller, Martin. "When the Nazis Came."

Paine, Thomas. "The American Crisis."

Peabody, Josephine Preson. "Icarus and Daedalus." *Old Greek Folk Stories Told Anew*. Boston: Houghton Mifflin Company, 1897.

———. "Odysseus and the Sirens." *Old Greek Folk Stories Told Anew*. Boston: Houghton Mifflin Company, 1897.

Robinson, Edwin Arlington. "Richard Cory."

Roosevelt, Theodore. "The Man in the Arena." The Sorbonne, Paris. April 23, 1910. Speech.

———. "The Strenuous Life." Hamilton Club. Chicago. April 10, 1899. Speech.

Shakespeare, William. "St. Crispin Day's Speech." *Henry V*.

Tennyson, Alfred. "Crossing the Bar."

Tolstoy, Leo. "How Much Land Does a Man Need?"

Wordsworth, William. "Daffodils."

ABOUT THE AUTHORS

JEFF SANDEFER is an entrepreneur, a teacher, and an educational innovator. As an entrepreneur, he started his first company at age sixteen. He recently sold his company, Sandefer Capital Partners, an energy investment firm with several billion dollars in assets. Jeff, along with his wife Laura, established Acton Academy, a low-cost elementary school that has been drawing national attention as one of the leaders in blended- and project-based learning. Jeff has been a longtime board member of *National Review* magazine, the Texas Public Policy Foundation, the Philanthropy Roundtable, and the Harvard Business School. He belongs to the Mont Pelerin Society and is one of the youngest people ever elected to the Texas Business Hall of Fame. He and Laura have three children, Taite, Charlie, and Sam.

REV. ROBERT A. SIRICO is a parish priest and author of *Defending the Free Market*. As president of the Acton Institute for the Study of Religion and Liberty, he has spoken to Catholic, Orthodox, and Protestant groups, to secular and religious university audiences, and to pastors and political leaders around the world. A tireless defender of economic freedom and entrepreneurship, Rev. Sirico emphasizes that God made us to be free, creative, and responsible, and any system that undermines that purpose will also undermine human flourishing. His essays have appeared in the *New York Times*, *National Review*, *Crisis*, *Forbes*, and the *Wall Street Journal*.

CPSIA information can be obtained
at www.ICGtesting.com
Printed in the USA
FFOW01n0808130116
20406FF